BLACKPOOL FC
Miscellany

BLACKPOOL FC
Miscellany

*Seasiders Trivia,
History, Facts & Stats*

GERRY WOLSTENHOLME

BLACKPOOL FC
Miscellany

© Gerry Wolstenholme, 2011

Gerry Wolstenholme has asserted his rights in accordance with the Copyright,
Designs and Patents Act 1988 to be identified as the author of this work.

Published By:
Know the Score Books
A2 Yeoman Gate
Yeoman Way
Durrington
BN13 3QZ

Email: info@pitchpublishing.co.uk
Web: www.pitchpublishing.co.uk

First published 2011

A catalogue record for this book is available from the British Library.

13-digit ISBN: 978-1-9054117-3-3

Typesetting and origination by Know the Score Books. Printed in Great Britain.
Manufacturing managed by Jellyfish Print Solutions Ltd.

FOREWORD BY IAN EVATT

I came to Blackpool Football Club in August 2006 from Queens Park Rangers, where things weren't going too well as I couldn't settle in London. Then out of the blue, Simon Grayson rang me and said that Blackpool were going to have a push for promotion in the forthcoming season and that a Latvian chap, who we now know as Valery Belokon, was going to put plenty of money into the club to enable Simon to start again and bring a new squad of players in.

Simon wanted me to come to Blackpool on loan, have a look at the set-up and perhaps become a part of it. It was something of a gamble because at the time Blackpool had just managed to avoid relegation from League One but I decided that it was worth that gamble. I came up here and for the first two games Wes Hoolahan and me sat on the bench and played very little part in successive defeats. After that I went to see Simon and asked him if I was going to play. He put me in for the next game against Bristol City, we won 4-2 and that was the beginning of an incredible season.

Eleven or 12 new players were brought in, we all started gelling and we went from bottom of the table after ten games to be pushing for automatic promotion. In the end, after an amazing ten successive victories, we got promoted at Wembley and that was something spectacular.

The second season was mainly about consolidating our position in the Championship and we managed to stay up quite comfortably. The team spirit that was engendered, with everyone getting on like a house on fire, and being very good friends on and off the pitch was something I had never before experienced. And it is something that has continued to the present day.

After that, of course, Ian Holloway arrived at the club and here we are now sat proudly in the Premier League two years later; it is incredible. Funnily enough 'Ollie' was my manager at Queens Park Rangers but he was completely different from what he is now. Then he was a committed 4-4-2 manager, a 'kick it along' person but when he later left Leicester City he had a think about things and decided that he had to have a new battle plan. He watched Spain and Barcelona and when he came to tell the players of his plans we all looked at him as though he was an alien. We just couldn't believe that we could play that way but the proof of the pudding is there for all to see as we are still improving.

We reached the play-offs and then winning at Wembley was magnificent. There's something very special about the club and for me as a player, in my fifth season, winning twice at Wembley and playing in the top flight was absolutely amazing. I am one of the lucky ones and this place is something very special – the aim as I write is to get back into the Premier League.

As for the history of the club, we are all interested as we often have the great Jimmy Armfield calling in to see us and discussing the past and, of course, we are all well aware of some of the great players such as Jimmy Hampson, Alan Suddick, Tony Green and, of course, the legendary Stan Matthews that have graced Bloomfield Road.

This book covers much of Blackpool's glorious and entertaining past and, like the current Blackpool side, I am certain that it will be a sure-fire winner.

INTRODUCTION

Blackpool football supporters are a hardy bunch. They have to be because the club's performances, sometimes magnificent, sometimes infuriatingly frustrating, and the associated activities can certainly make the heart flutter. And the tangerine blood coursing through the veins often flows like molten lava. However, despite this predicament there is no doubt that once a Blackpool supporter, always a Blackpool supporter.

I took that step as a youngster, following in the footsteps of my Dad who was brought up on such players as Harry Mingay, Harry Bedford, Jimmy Hampson, 'Jock' Dodds and the two Stanleys, Matthews and Mortensen. He would delight in regaling me with tales of derring-do in the days of yore and these fuelled my interest in the history of the club and its players.

I attended reserve games with my Dad, first-team games attracted too many spectators for a small boy to see properly, before being allowed to attend on my own as a nine-year old. My first game sealed my admiration for the men in tangerine as it was a resounding 5-1 victory over Newcastle United so thereafter I rarely missed a game, sitting often, in the days of crowds of more than 30,000, on the cinder track behind the goal at the Spion Kop end.

I have since spent many happy hours watching Blackpool and also many hours in gathering together various snippets of information that fascinated me about the club. Some of these are included here and cover a wide spectrum, being poignant, exhilarating, amusing and downright bizarre.

To use one of the manager's words, I hope that you find this a belter of a book and enjoy the reading of it as much as I have enjoyed its compilation.

Gerry Wolstenholme
January 2011

COLOURFUL CHARACTERS

The Atomic Boys were a group of devoted Blackpool supporters seen regularly on football grounds around the country from the late 1940s through to the early 1960s. The Atomic Boys were the brainchild of keen Blackpool supporter Syd Bevers who, at a replayed cup tie against Middlesbrough on 4 February 1946, thought "there was a distinct lack of colour" at the game. He soon changed things and the exotically dressed Atomic Boys were formed. Many of their costumes were borrowed from Louis Tussaud's waxworks and for a number of years Syd had a duck, which served as Blackpool's mascot. Over the years there was Donald, Puskas and Douglas, the last named presented by Douglas Fairbanks, Jr. Against the advice of Stan Matthews, who suggested that there was no way a duck could be sneaked into Wembley, Syd even managed to get the duck in for the 1953 FA Cup Final and what's more he paraded it around the touchline too!

MORE SPECTATORS?

On 5 May 1949 Blackpool Football Club were putting forward plans to a Blackpool Corporation Sub-Committee to increase the capacity of the Bloomfield Road ground from 31,422 to 64,964 at an estimated cost of £350,000. The work was planned for two stages. Stage one would see the capacity increased to 47,205 and would cost £114,000 with the work including a new upper tier in the West Stand, increasing the capacity from 3,065 to 8,318, increased standing in the West Paddock, 3,242 to 3,786, re-stepping the Spion Kop with a halfway level entrance, which would add 1,294, a new stand on the east side, increasing capacity from 6,700 to 15,036, and re-stepping the South Paddock, an increase from 900 to 3,373. Stage two, taking the capacity up to 64,964, would cost over £200,000 and would include an additional 1,313 seats and 507 standing spaces in the South Paddock, new rooms for officials and a refreshment provision under the West Stand. The overall capacity would then be 14,681 seated and 49,313 standing. The planners estimated that the crowd would be clear of the ground in around 12 to 15 minutes. No discussion was held on how the money to fund the development would be raised but the football club thought it a better scheme than one costing £1,250,000 that the Town Council had originally suggested. The plan never materialised.

GET THAT BALL!

In the 1978/79 season Blackpool secretary Wilf Smith decided that there should be ball boys at Bloomfield Road to field the stray balls that went out of play. It seemed a relatively simple task to recruit them from local sports clubs and boys' clubs but the task of doing so dragged on for quite some time. In March 1979 yet another snag cropped up after the Blackpool Schools FA had worked out a rota for two dozen boys who had volunteered to do the job. Smith felt that the proposal would probably have to wait until the 1979/80 season because, he said, "We need somewhere for the lads to have a shower after a wet day. Unfortunately we have no changing area for them. I want to do the job properly. I don't want lads getting soaked, going home unchanged or unshowered and being off school with flu." He did add that he did not intend the scheme to be dropped. In August 1979 tracksuits had been ordered for the local youngsters who had expressed an interest and on 17 August Smith commented, "I think we can overcome the problem of a changing room and I hope to give the lads the go-ahead in the next week or so."

TICKETS ONLY PLEASE

The first all-ticket game at Bloomfield Road was against Blackburn Rovers on Boxing Day 1946. A crowd of 25,576 saw the only goal of the game by Stan Mortensen win the match for Blackpool.

TAKE YOUR PARTNERS

When Blackpool won promotion to the First Division after the 1929/30 season there was a grand victory ball at the Tower Ballroom on 7 May 1930. The players were immortalised by having all the dances of the evening named after them. There was 'Wil-son always shine', 'Percival's Delight', 'Tough-Nell', 'Wolfe guards his den', 'Pearson's Special', 'Take Oxo and prevent those Quinn-sies', 'What will the Ram-say?', 'Our Dreams have come true, Tremelling in the moonlight', 'Grant me this one', 'Hampson tiptoes through the defences', 'Ure my Lady love', 'Jazz' mania', 'Broadhurst's volleys', 'I'm Bent on you', 'Ups and Downes', 'Charles' Paradise', 'Bar Bar Black Croft', 'Wats-on next?', 'I Upt-on at em', 'Laud-O'-Dale', 'Be He Rich-eh' and 'Neal and Pray'.

CHANNON FOR MANAGER?

After Bob Stokoe left the club by mutual consent on 17 August 1979, Mike Channon, then unsettled at Manchester City, was installed as one of the favourites to take over at Blackpool as player-manager. He was left out of the season opener by City and attended Bloomfield Road to watch Blackpool beat Gillingham 2-1 and further fuel speculation that he was in line for an appointment at the club. On 22 August it was said that he had a 50-50 chance of taking over as player-manager and he had an interview with the Blackpool board. He commented, "I want to get into management and I think it is best to start in the lower divisions and Blackpool is the right club to start. But I have to consider offers from First Division clubs and weigh my desires to get into management with my desire to prove my ability as a First Division footballer. Blackpool have pointed out to me that I may not get as good a chance in a couple of years if I decide to continue playing in the top flight, and obviously that is something I have to consider very seriously. Opportunities have to be grasped, but going from a First Division player to a Third Division player-manager is a really big move and one I have to think about most carefully. Last night's defeat [3-0 by Bury] did not put me off. They played well to beat Gillingham in the first match." Channon eventually decided to decline any offer from Blackpool and continued playing.

NO CONFLICT OF INTEREST

At a meeting of the General Purposes Committee of Blackpool Town Council in October 1935 a resolution was passed, with only one dissention, that members of Blackpool Town Council who were also shareholders of Blackpool Football Club would be allowed to debate and subsequently vote on matters of finance appertaining to the football club. This reversed a decision taken the previous year when such personnel were not permitted to debate or vote on football club matters. The issue had arisen again because the football club were appealing for their grant of £500 to be increased to £2,000 as the directors felt that Blackpool as a town benefited greatly from the publicity generated by the club and it was, therefore, deemed to be well worth the higher figure.

BEHIND CLOSED DOORS

A most unlikely event took place on 13 December 1961 when Blackpool played Arsenal in a behind-closed-doors friendly game at the Squires Gate practice ground. Arsenal, who were staying in Blackpool at the Norbreck Hydro prior to playing Burnley on the following Saturday, played their first team including Eddie Clamp, Henderson, Charles, Eastham, Kelsey, and Laurie Brown while Blackpool played a mainly reserve team. Arsenal, not surprisingly, won 2-0 but Blackpool manager Ronnie Suart commented, "Our reserve players did very well and I'm sure it did them good to play against first-class opposition." Arsenal's manager George Swindin said, "It gave us a chance to experiment and it was a useful departure from the normal training routine."

GROUND IMPROVEMENTS

For the start of the 1908/09 season the Bloomfield Road ground had been widened and a grandstand to hold 5,000 spectators had been built on the railway [west] side of the ground, which was then expected to have a 16-18,000 capacity. One spectator's comment was: "The general improvement of the ground is most satisfactory, and in itself should attract many new supporters."

A CLOSE SHAVE

Mr Jesse Smith Turner, known to sports fans everywhere as the 'Razor Blade King', died in Wesham Park Hospital aged 76 on 13 February 1977. He had lived in retirement at his home in Castle Avenue, Carleton with his wife Clarissa. Born in Rochdale he had sold razor blades at all but two of the English Football League grounds, every Rugby League ground, every racecourse in the country and all the Test match cricket venues. He had also visited Wembley on 60 occasions. On some Saturdays he used to visit two Lancashire venues selling his razor blades and he had appeared on radio and television talking about his unusual career. He was often seen at Bloomfield Road in the days when the crowds were in excess of 25,000 and consequently his takings were enormous.

ADVERTISING PAYS

Mr G Furber, a signwriter, of Brunswick Street and St Chad's Road, secured the advertising rights at Bloomfield Road for the 15th consecutive season in 1924/25.

TITLE SUCCESS

Blackpool's record of played 16, won 11, drawn 3, lost 2, goals for 44, goals against 24, points 25, gave them the Northern Mid-Week League title in the 1931/32 season. It was the club's first success in a minor league competition since the Central League championship was won in 1919/20.

UNFAIR CRITICISM

In September 1925 a section of the crowd at Bloomfield Road constantly barracked the reserve team players and the club's official comment was: "This unfair and unsportsmanlike conduct by some of the spectators is giving our players a good deal of anxiety. The lads are made so nervous by the remarks passed among the spectators that they are put off their usual game. Away from home they have played much better than at Bloomfield Road, and this is attributable to the conduct of the spectators at Bloomfield Road. Spectators should remember that the players are doing their best, and instead of being discouraged, they ought to be encouraged. To encourage them, and to overlook occasional slips, is the best way of developing the youngster. Our players are complaining of the things said about them by some of the fans at Bloomfield Road. This is a serious and lamentable state of affairs."

LIVE ON TELEVISION

The Blackpool versus Bolton Wanderers game on 10 September 1960 was the first Football League match to be televised live with the kick-off put back to the early evening. ITV billed the programme as *The Big Match* and cinema managers and owners of public houses complained about a slump in business that evening as a viewing audience of 2,350,000, the largest in league history to that time, watched Blackpool lose 1-0 to a goal by Freddie Hill. Unfortunately the game was no thriller and perhaps because of this, the series was not deemed worth continuing with and no further games were shown!

NO DUCKS ALLOWED

The Blackpool FC mascot Douglas the duck was barred from Bloomfield Road in April 1952 and was made available to any responsible person who would give a suitable donation to charity. The leader of the Atomic Boys, Syd Bevers, said, "I had an offer from supporters of a Scottish club. I had another offer from a man who wanted to exhibit Douglas in a Central Beach sideshow but that was turned down flat." In the end Douglas had a vacation on a Poulton-le-Fylde farm and Bevers understood Blackpool's action in banning Douglas. He commented, "The duck idea has been played out. I think it was a good idea though, for while we had the ducks we raised £800 for charity and distributed thousands of leaflets advertising Blackpool. We'll have thought of something else by next season." He did – another duck!

PROGRAMME OR TEAMSHEET?

Blackpool launched a sales drive at their first home match of the 1976/77 season against Burnley in the Anglo-Scottish Cup on 11 August 1976. The programme, which had lost money all of the previous seasons, was to contain new features and commercial manager Bob Waite hoped that the revival of interest in club affairs since the takeover by the new board and the interim signing of striker Bob Hatton would be reflected in programme sales for the forthcoming season. If this did not transpire in the early games, he was prepared to scrap an official match programme and issue just a teamsheet to cut the club's losses. Colour was to be introduced for the first time and consequently the programme would cost 5p more at 15p and Blackpool had to sell 1,800 out of a print run of 3,000 to make a profit. In the whole of the 1975/76 season programme sales were only 60,000 as gates slumped to an average 8,000. Of the total programme sales, 12,000 were sold at the FA Cup tie against Burnley when there was a crowd of 21,000. Mr Waite commented, "In everything we are doing we are aiming for the First Division. So the programme will be geared to that end. I am here to make a profit wherever possible and to cut our losses where there is no market. I am sure the spectators will rally round and find that our programme is as good as any."

CLOTHING COUPONS

On 1 November 1943 the Blackpool directors were expecting an allocation from 40,000 clothing coupons that were available for football clubs to replace 'outfits'. A club official said, "We are just managing with our equipment and we anticipate a coupon allotment to help us to renew that which is worn out. It is only because we had fair supplies at the outbreak of war that we have bought nothing since the war broke out. We have assisted many service teams when they were short of equipment."

BLACKPOOL LIGHTS

Blackpool first appeared in a floodlit game on 30 May 1951 when they played Grasshoppers of Zurich on their close season tour and it was a successful debut as they won 4-3.

BAD BOYS

Blackpool manager Bob Stokoe and chairman Frank Dickinson attended an FA Disciplinary Committee meeting in London on 10 August 1971 to answer for the club's poor disciplinary record during the 1970/71 season. The club received 30 bookings for players of all the club's sides, 25 of these were before Stokoe took over as manager. The club finished third bottom of the Ford Sporting League with only Millwall and Bolton Wanderers below them. Fortunately, no action was taken and after the hearing Stokoe commented, "I shall be telling the players before the season starts that we expect an improvement this season. It was an informal meeting yesterday and the FA appreciated the fact that it was a troubled year for the club and that I was the third manager in a year and not all of it was my responsibility. But it was particularly disturbing that there were 13 bookings in the Lancashire League involving our players. This is a bad trend among young players and every effort will be made to improve the disciplinary record next season."

ANFIELD SUCCESS

On the opening day of the season, 18 August 1962, goals from Ray Charnley and Des Horne gave Blackpool a 2-1 victory, inflicting on Liverpool their first league home defeat since 31 December 1960.

THE DEAL THAT NEVER WAS

Blackpool and Arsenal agreed terms for Tommy Docherty, the 32-year-old wing-half on 7 October 1960 and he was selected to play for the Seasiders against Fulham the following day. Blackpool manager Ronnie Suart commented, "We know that Docherty is not young, but we feel that he has the experience to be of considerable help, and there is no doubt that he puts tremendous bite and enthusiasm into his play." The fee was not stated but it was believed to be "near the five-figure mark". However, the transfer broke down when Docherty refused to move and Suart remarked, "He was offered a part-time job in Blackpool and the chance of coaching appointments but he would not change his mind."

BOUNCING BALL

Blackpool had been chasing Alan Ball to be the successor to Stan Ternent for some time but so had Jack Charlton, the Sheffield Wednesday manager and Ball's former England team-mate. Indeed, Charlton was confident that Ball would join him at Hillsborough as player-coach and said so to the press. Then when he heard very strong rumours that Ball was to join Blackpool on 19 February 1980 he was reportedly annoyed but he was still confident of getting his man so he announced, "I have not heard from 'Bally' whom I spoke to last week and this gives me great hope because it means he has not signed anything for Blackpool. There has been a lot of speculation, but until he signs for Blackpool I am confident he has got our message." Blackpool, who were close to sealing the deal with Ball, were incensed and issued an official statement the same day that stated, "It is officially confirmed that Alan Ball has already agreed terms with Blackpool Football Club in connection with his job as player-manager. He is in constant touch with Blackpool directors and is already working on certain aspects of his new post. He tried to contact Jack Charlton twice yesterday but was not successful and he will be trying again to get in touch today to quell any rumours concerning joining Sheffield Wednesday." Ball duly signed a three-year contract with Blackpool on 29 February 1980 but, by a bizarre quirk of fate that had already committed him to Tony Waiters and his Vancouver Whitecaps in Canada, did not take up his post until July 1980.

ROOMS REQUIRED

When former player Jackie Wright was appointed chief scout at Blackpool in the 1973/74 season one of his most important jobs was to find accommodation for the young apprentices that the club signed and for players brought to Bloomfield Road for trials. The club felt strongly that getting settled in and becoming contented members of the squad was an important factor in the youngsters' development so Wright advertised in the programme for any help that he could get under the heading 'Mums wanted for our 'Pool stars of the future'. In January 1974 he wrote, "During the coming months Blackpool will be very active compiling their list of associate schoolboys … This means that from the age of 14 there will be a number of youths on our register … their next step will be to become Blackpool apprentice professionals … these prospects come to Bloomfield Road from all parts of the country … I am seeking for them as much suitable accommodation as I can obtain, where lads will live in 'digs' in a happy, family atmosphere. Blackpool FC's wish is for them to enjoy comfortable, friendly rooms where they will quickly become one of the household. Some will be living away from their parents for the first time." He ended with a plea, "Accordingly, I would be grateful to hear from anyone who may be able to offer the type of accommodation we require or from anyone who may know any other families prepared to find our young footballers a home-from-home." Many of Blackpool's youngsters were housed in this way and many of them kept in touch with the families who looked after them after they had graduated to become full-time professionals and even after they had moved on from the club.

REPUTATIONS COUNT FOR NOTHING

When leading the Second Division, their highest position since becoming a league club, Blackpool, who had opened the season with a 10-game undefeated run to that point, were knocked out of the English [FA] Cup in the fourth qualifying round, losing 2-1 to Lancashire League club Darwen on 17 November 1900. It was the start of a decline in fortunes because the club finally finished in 12th place, winning only seven games and drawing two after the disastrous cup result.

MUSIC FOR THE CHARTS!

The Nolan Sisters, who were resident in Blackpool, recorded a song entitled 'Blackpool' for the football club supporters in 1976 and even though Joe Harris penned a rival in 'The Seasiders', commercial manager Bob Waite was adamant that the Nolans' song was the only one for Blackpool Football Club. The club ordered 300 copies of the record at the start of the season and by mid-October 1976 had sold out. Mr Waite commented, "As a professional commercial manager I believe that it is in the interests of everybody connected with the club that the current song is continued. It has been accepted as the official club song and that is an end to the matter. People can stop putting pen to paper to come up with an alternative now the record is already a success. I would urge anyone who has energy to spare to use it in supporting the club by becoming Tote agents and giving us every support. The board have done their bit. Two bargain signings have cost them a great deal of money and every fan should now work to reward the board for their efforts." Joe Harris had already penned one song that the football club had used up to the previous season and he felt that his offering, 'Tangerine and White', had brought the club some luck. The chorus of his latest song was "We'll follow, follow, follow the Seasiders,/Everyone will shout about the Seasiders,/Here, there and everywhere,/We're right behind the Seasiders."

SWEEPING CHANGES

Two weeks after Colin Greenall had made his debut as Blackpool's youngest ever league player and a week after Eamonn Collins had appeared in the Anglo-Scottish Cup against Kilmarnock to become Blackpool's youngest ever senior player, both boys found themselves sweeping out the dressing rooms. Manager Alan Ball laughingly commented to anyone within earshot, "You remember these lads, don't you?" The two youngsters took it in good part and continued their chores with pleasure and enthusiasm, just delighted to be a part of the first-team atmosphere.

A NEW TRAINER

Will Moran of Rotherham was the new trainer appointed by Blackpool on 11 May 1923 possibly because he had previously worked with Blackpool manager Bill Norman at Barnsley.

INSTANT DISMISSAL

Two Blackpool players have been sent off on their league debuts for the club. Kevin Tully received his marching orders against Burnley on 26 December 1972 and Charlie Adam was dismissed against Doncaster Rovers on 7 February 2009. Blackpool lost both games, 2-1 to Burnley and 3-2 to Doncaster.

LOST IN THE WASH

Against Bristol City on 7 September 1901 Blackpool played in a new strip rather than the previously used blue and white stripes. The press comment was "No longer can Blackpool be referred to as the stripes for they have changed their attire and whoever first suggested the new colours deserves to be complimented. The jerseys are a pretty light blue, and the knickers a rich navy, and the neat, clean appearance of the men as they entered the lists was very favourably commented upon, everybody apparently being well satisfied with the change." However the players were not wearing light blue strip for long because on the first washing of the kit, the blue dye disappeared and the shirts became white thus Blackpool continued to play in white shirts and navy shorts for some time and became know as 'The Lilywhites'.

BLACKBOARD TACTICS

When manager of Blackpool in August 1923 Major Frank Buckley was to "inaugurate a course of blackboard instructions, and to deal with some of the best means of getting out of difficult positions without losing too much advantage", one critic reported,:"In short, it may be said that Major Buckley believes in science as well as muscle in football, or brains as well as brawn, and every supporter of the club will wish him success in his methods."

NO FEES

Blackpool was the only club that did not pay any agents' fees in the 12 months between July 2007 and June 2008. Leicester City were the biggest spenders with £1,630,287 but Blackpool contributed not a penny to the £11.1 million cumulative spend.

VERY NEARLY SHANKLY

Blackpool's directors asked Bill Shankly if he would manager the club until the end of the 1977/78 season on 9 February 1978 following the controversial dismissal of Allan Brown. The directors had appointed Jimmy Meadows to the post as a caretaker-manager but they said that they wanted an experienced hand "to guide the trouble-torn ship through stormy waters". The 63-year-old Shankly was at the time working in an advisory capacity at Third Division Wrexham and he preferred not to comment, stating only, "I would be happier if you would get any statement at this stage from Blackpool." The Blackpool directors had decided that they did not want to rush into any permanent appointment as the season was nearly over and this announcement was made: "The appointment we make must be with the long term future in mind and we do not want to jump in as we feel we can make a first-class appointment. What we need is a steadying hand and Bill Shankly fits the bill. Otherwise we are confident that Jimmy Meadows will do a very capable job until the position is filled permanently." Meadows had moved to Carleton to make travel to Bloomfield Road easier and had no contract as he said it was "not essential for managers". When Shankly gave Blackpool a polite "No, thank you", although he was "flattered by the offer", Meadows was confirmed as temporary manager.

A SWEET TOOTH!

"Sweets at the match?" That was the question in May 1949 when the answer was "Not yet" after permits for the sale of sweets at both Blackpool Football Club's ground and Blackpool Cricket Club's ground were refused at a meeting of the Blackpool Food Control Committee on 5 May 1949. Chairman of the committee Councillor C Dunn said that as Blackpool Football Club was to close for the summer, and as there was a sweet shortage, it was decided there would be no harm in the application being left to a later date! The proposal to sell sweets at Blackpool Cricket Club's ground was defeated by six votes to five as it was decided to wait until de-rationing had settled down and there was more evidence of consumer need. The chairman stressed that the cricket club was not being singled out as a large number of applications had been refused!

THE BEST IS NOT TO COME

There were strong rumours afoot that when George Best returned from America and was awaiting clearance to play for Fulham in September 1976, Blackpool made him an offer to join them. Some time later Best's then wife, Angela MacDonald James-Best commented, "Blackpool made a bid but it did not do much for George. We are quite happy to wait and see what happens. George isn't unduly bothered whether he plays football or not." And then she delivered a kick in the teeth to Blackpool when she added, "But when he makes a comeback he wants to play for a good team, not go to Blackpool or some dumb place that wants to buy a big name."

ANYTHING FOR A GOOD VIEW

There was a tremendous crowd at the top-of-the-table Lancashire League clash between Blackpool and Bury at Raikes Hall on 21 October 1893 when "all points of vantage were taken up, the stand against the theatre being brought into requisition, while the incomplete building which was intended for a representation of Niagara Falls was largely used by enterprising enthusiasts who did not object to a little climbing so long as a good view of the game was procured". Ninety minutes before the kick-off there were many "lively scenes around the Royal Palace Gardens" and turnstiles were blocked as people pushed and shoved to get in. Blackpool won 2-0 and the gate receipts were a massive £112 14s 0d.

A DIRTY BUSINESS

Blackpool were fined £800 after the 1979/80 season for accumulating 250 disciplinary points during the season. And the following season they accumulated 197 points and had to face an FA Disciplinary Committee on 25 August 1981 when chairman Ken Chadwick simply said, "We will probably be fined." In that 1980/81 season the manager Alan Ball had decided that the club would not fine sinners and in four months up to November 1980, 120 disciplinary points were accumulated, including eight bookings for dissent. The board then stepped in and insisted on fines for players being restored and only another 77 points were accrued during the remainder of the season and there was then only one booking for dissent – and that for Alan Ball!

A GAME IN PROGRESS AT RAIKES HALL GARDENS IN THE MID-1890s.

LEARNING THE TRADE

Blackpool employed 12 apprentices for the 1977/78 season and only Newcastle United with 13 had more while Chelsea were the only other club with 12.

COLD ... BRR ... BRR

In the winter of 1962/63 Blackpool played no home games between 15 December 1962 and 2 March 1963 due to what was called the big freeze. In that time they played two games away from Bloomfield Road, at White Hart Lane and Old Trafford, as most football was postponed over the period. The FA Cup third round tie against Norwich City at Carrow Road was also a casualty and it was postponed 11 times, being played at the 12th time of asking on 4 March 1963. In an attempt to get the game played, the Carrow Road pitch was treated with flamethrowers on 22 January 1963 as, according to a Norwich spokesman, "a last desperate effort". However they "served no purpose whatsoever" for "as fast as the ice melted it froze again". An icebreaker was also used but it too proved ineffective. At Bloomfield Road Jimmy Armfield and Tony Waiters ice-skated on the pitch on 8 January 1963 and two days later Barrie Martin, 'Mandy' Hill and two other players joined them. On 29 January 1963 Blackpool used a disc harrow to try to get the game against West Ham United played on 2 February 1963 but that too proved ineffective and on 30 January 1963 the players swept a heavy fall of snow from the pitch in the vain hope that it would be clear underneath but the ice, one to four inches thick, was "as formidable as ever".

JOB OPPORTUNITIES

In February 1980 a Small Business Centre was set up at Blackpool and the Fylde College to encourage the growth of such enterprises and anyone interested was invited to attend training courses that could be from two days to 15 weeks in length. One of the first to welcome the idea and to express an interest was Blackpool goalkeeper Iain Hesford who said, "There are too many footballers today who spend all their money as they earn it and then end up working on the factory floor. I'll be going on the course."

LOANED FROM LYTHAM

A new ground was found for the Blackpool 'A' team in March 1948, as an enclosed ground was required. It was the Lytham FC ground at Ballam Road and the club were to use it from the 1948/49 season onwards with the arrangements being that Blackpool would assist in putting the playing area in good order and subsequently help with the maintenance and that they would also lend amateur players on their staff to Lytham should that club require them. In addition Lytham players, particularly those living in Blackpool, could call in at Bloomfield Road for treatment to injuries. The gate money from the new venture would go to Blackpool who would meet all expenses when they played there. Lytham would continue to have priority in such instances as cup ties with Blackpool regarded as "the guest team".

THIEVES IN THE NIGHT

There was a burglary at Bloomfield Road on the night of 8 September 1907. An iron bar was used to break in and all the doors were broken open. Footballs and foot pumps were taken and other articles were thrown about the dressing rooms and tents. No-one was caught for the robbery.

MATCH ABANDONED - VERY NEARLY

Blackpool's football newspaper *The Green* reported 'Pool Draw After Riot' following the 2-2 draw with Wolves at Bloomfield Road on 30 October 1976. Missile-hurling fans caused the game to be stopped when they threw stones onto the field, hitting Blackpool goalkeeper George Wood on the hand five minutes into the second half. Referee Walter Johnson of Kendal took the players off the field for five minutes and issued a stern warning to fans that he would abandon the game if there were a repetition of the action – and there was no further trouble.

SIGN PLEASE

After Blackpool had lost 1-0 to Blackburn Rovers in the Cumberland Cup at Workington on 4 May 1949, 1,000 youngsters invaded the pitch in an attempt to get Stan Mortensen's autograph. 'Morty' had to be rescued and escorted from the field by police.

BRIBERY AND CORRUPTION

A Manchester newspaper report on the Blackpool versus Everton game on 12 January 1918 read, "It is alleged that last week an attempt was made to bribe players of the Everton club to lose their home game with Blackpool. Everton's reply was to win by seven goals to two. It is understood that the matter has been reported to the governing body, and an enquiry will be held today [Wednesday 16 January] at Manchester." A joint commission of the Football Association and the Football League met at the Grand Hotel, Manchester regarding alleged attempts to 'square' the Oldham Athletic versus Blackburn Rovers, Manchester United versus Burnley and Everton versus Blackpool games. The result was "Several players and officials of Everton were called before the Commission and Mr W Cuff, the secretary, produced 20 £1 notes, which, it was alleged, had been handed to four of the Everton players on the understanding that Blackpool did not lose the game with Everton at Goodison Park last Saturday. Manchester United and Burnley also offered their decision. George Anderson the Manchester United forward was called but he was unable to attend. Sufficient evidence has been produced before George Anderson, and which he had the fullest opportunity of answering, to justify the Commission in suspending him sine die, but they are not able to dispose of the charges and arrive at a final decision until Anderson has had the opportunity of replying to further material evidence. Anderson is therefore suspended sine die from playing or taking part in football." Nothing came of the allegations against Blackpool and Everton.

ELLIS TIMES TWO

Blackpool's Lancashire Cup tie against Preston North End on 26 July 1994 had a little added spice in that two of Blackpool's new recruits, ironically with the same surname, were pitted against their former club in their home debut. Manager Sam Ellis and striker Tony Ellis were both signed from 'Pool's nearest rivals. Sam had been youth coach at Deepdale after having been overlooked for the manager's job when John Beck was appointed, so he was pleased to get his first managerial appointment in England. Tony, a North End goal hero, agreed a three-year deal with the Seasiders and then a tribunal fixed the fee at £165,000, Blackpool's record at the time. Ellis, Tony that is, scored Blackpool's goal in a 1-1 draw.

JUNIORS AT LYTHAM

The Blackpool 'B' team, managed by assistant manager Sam Jones, played at Lytham FC's ground at Ballam Road in the late 1940s/early 1950s. For this facility Blackpool paid Lytham £150 per year but in February 1955 there was talk of the side moving to the newly refurbished "pavilion and football pitch" at Squires Gate. But Mr Jones eased Lytham's fears by stating that the new facility was "to be used by the Colts side and for training the junior and young professional players". In the financial position Lytham were in at the time, the loss of the £150 would have been disastrous.

SELFISH SOUTH SHORE

Having lost their place in the Football League Division Two after finishing third from bottom in the 1898/99 season, Blackpool Football Club applied to rejoin the Lancashire League. And, "despite the unsportsmanlike conduct of South Shore in opposing them" they were elected as a member for the 1899/1900 season. At the meeting when their application was discussed, "The South Shore representative spoke for a considerable time against the inclusion of Blackpool and then finished up by registering his vote accordingly." One of the local football reporters thought the attitude of South Shore was "selfish" and he was "surprised that the rulers of the South Shore club could stoop to it". He stated, "They forget there are people at the north end of town who want to see a football match. But he wanted them to journey down to Waterloo Road to see a game." He added he felt their action "would forever stand in the way of amalgamation and having a good central ground". And his final word on the subject was "It will be a fight to the death now. Which club will last the longer?" The answer to that was soon to be revealed when, in December 1899, South Shore withdrew from the league and the club amalgamated with Blackpool.

NOT FOR SALE

In September 1930 the Blackpool Council offered the sum of £500 for some land in Bloomfield Road that belonged to the football club but at a directors' meeting on 11 September it was decided that the club could not accept the offer and they wrote to the council accordingly.

SOS

With Blackpool in severe financial difficulties in the summer of 1983 a Save Blackpool Appeal Fund was set up to help alleviate the club's problems. Meetings were held at which Brian London and Glyn James were guest speakers but the main event of the campaign was an Old Blackpool versus Old Liverpool game at Bloomfield Road on 7 August 1983. There were 3,000 spectators present to see Liverpool win 5-3 with the Blackpool goals coming from Sam Ellis, Alan Suddick and Ray Pointer. The Liverpool players generously gave their services free and their very strong side included Ian St John, Tommy Smith, Ron Yeats and Ian Callaghan and had comedian Russ Abbot in goal. Owen Oyston paid £100 into the fund so that he could play for the Old Blackpool side and with money raised from the open day at Bloomfield Road that preceded the game, a sum of £3,000 was added to the kitty. Later in the month the sum of £4,600 had been raised and the fund's chairman, Stuart Thompson, presented a cheque for that amount to club chairman Ken Chadwick. In accepting the cheque, Mr Chadwick said, "I am humbled by the hard work the fans have put in to raise cash. The new players have remarked on the marvellous spirit and liaison that has sprung up between the club and the fans and we hope the reward for all concerned is promotion." Sadly it wasn't to be promotion as Blackpool finished the 1983/84 season in sixth place in Division Four.

AN EXPERIMENTAL SIDE

Blackpool played Manchester United at Bloomfield Road on 10 November 1909 in a friendly game that was arranged as part of the transfer deal that took Arthur Whalley from Bloomfield Road to Old Trafford. The game gave the directors "an opportunity of trying some interesting experiments in the arrangement of the team". The Blackpool side was Fiske, Gladwin, Whittingham, Connor, Golding, Clarke, Didymus, Beare, Slade, Elmore and Dawson. Centre-half Percy Golding was normally a full-back and played his 15 league and cup games for the club in that position, Donald Slade never made the first team in league or cup and Edward Didymus played only two league games for the club. Blackpool won the game 3-2 with the goals coming from Beare, Connor and goalkeeper 'Tommy' Fiske from a penalty.

GENEROSITY NOT REPAID

The Bury directors generously agreed that their club would play Blackpool in a friendly game at Raikes Hall on 25 February 1899 with a minimum of expenses "for excursion fares and teas" in recompense. Blackpool repaid their kindness by winning 3-2!

A MODEST INCREASE

Blackpool's average attendance in the 1997/98 season was 5,220 compared with 4,987 the previous season, an increase of 4.7 per cent. The highest attendance was 8,342 for the visit of Preston North End on 20 December and the lowest was 3,281, on a cold 2 December night, for the visit of Plymouth Argyle. Preston, who brought 2,485 fans with them, were beaten 2-1 while Plymouth, with 103 hardy souls as support, drew 0-0.

BALANCING THE BOOKS

Perhaps surprisingly in view of the lower attendances in the wartime season of 1918/19, Blackpool made a profit of £99 on the season. Gate receipts were £3,185 19s 0d and £560 was received as compensation for fire damage done to the West Stand. Total expenditure was £1,827 6s 2d with the largest single item being the £968 7s 0d expended on travel expenses and players' wages (which were minimal under wartime rules). Other expenses included £122 9s 4d spent on ground maintenance and repairs, £91 11s 0d on the trainer's wages and £57 11s 3d on referee and linesmen fees.

CRICKETING FOOTBALLERS

Blackpool Football Club played Preston North End Football Club at cricket on 10 August 1927. The game was a 12-a-side contest and Blackpool won by one wicket. Preston batted first and made 80 all out with the Leyland professional, Shakespeare, who Preston had drafted in, making 19 and W Sharples 20. Jimmy Hampson took 5-35, Peter Thorpe 3-20 and Wilf Slack 3-14. Blackpool won the game, replying with 85-10, the individual scores being, Bill Tremelling 11, George Ayres 6, Bill Benton 0, Syd Beaumont 4, Len Crompton 5, Matt Crook 22, Thorpe 18, Hampson 6, Reg Wright 4, Slack 0 not out and Percy Downes 6 with 3 extras.

THE ROAD TO WEMBLEY ...

Blackpool's first English [later FA] Cup tie was a first qualifying round tie on 3 October 1891 away at Higher Walton, one of their Lancashire League rivals. Two goals from both 'Gyp' Cookson and Billy Parkinson and one from Harry Davy gave Blackpool a 5-4 victory. Three further qualifying rounds were won, including a famous 4-3 victory over First Division Newton Heath (later Manchester United), and Blackpool were not disgraced when losing 3-0 to First Division Sheffield United in the first round proper.

WHERE DO I CALL HOME?

The only Blackpool footballer born at sea was goalkeeper Tommy Wilcox who first saw the light of day sometime in 1879 on the four-masted barque *Grassendale* that was sailing from the UK to the USA.

ONE MAN SHORT

For four successive games in the 2008/09 season Blackpool ended with ten men on the field, against Birmingham City, Queens Park Rangers, Crystal Palace and Doncaster Rovers. Keith Southern went off injured against Birmingham after the three substitutes had been used, Stephen Crainey, having gone on as a third substitute, had to retire injured against Queens Park Rangers, Paul Rachubka was sent off in the third minute against Crystal Palace and debutant Charlie Adam was sent off early in the second half against Doncaster. Blackpool beat Birmingham 2-0, lost 3-0 to QPR, beat Crystal Palace 1-0 and lost 3-2 to Doncaster.

SHORT-TERM APPOINTMENT

After taking over as caretaker from Bob Stokoe on the eve of the 1979/80 season, Stan Ternent was appointed on a permanent basis on 19 September 1979. The 33-year-old commented, "I'm happy to be given the chance and I can promise all-out effort for promotion." Chairman Bill Gregson said, "We have looked at it very carefully and Mr Ternent is the best man for the job. We're 100 per cent behind him." The vote of confidence was not to last long because, with Blackpool near the bottom of Division Three, Alan Ball replaced him in February 1980.

AN AUTOCRATIC VICAR

The Reverend Norman Stuart Jeffrey, vicar of St John's and president of Blackpool St John's Football Club, was an autocrat who refused to allow a change of name resolution that his St John's club become Blackpool Football Club to be put to a meeting of St John's players and supporters on 22 July 1887. He compared the situation to that of Parliament and the Queen, himself in the latter role and the club members in that of Parliament. In that allegory, nothing could be done without the Queen's consent and he had no intention of giving his consent to the proposal so he saw no point in putting the motion forward. He stressed that he would not abolish St John's denominational title and that he would endeavour to continue the club as a junior organisation if necessary. The members were, therefore, powerless to act and the 40 who desired the change adjourned to the next door Stanley Arms in Church Street and agreed to start, or if the previous Blackpool club (1877-1886) is acknowledged, restart, a Blackpool Football Club. Jeffrey had become vicar of St John's in 1868, he lost a leg in a street brawl that he tried to break up in 1891 and died at his residence Rylea in Thornton on 9 September 1919, aged 86. He was buried at Blackpool cemetery on 12 September 1919 with his main claim to fame being that he was instrumental, albeit unintentionally, in the forming of Blackpool Football Club as we know it today.

RECORDS LOST

On Sunday 13 January 1918 half of the grandstand at Bloomfield Road was destroyed by fire. The alarm was received at Central Police Station and the motor fire engine turned out under the superintendence of the Chief Constable Mr W J Pringle. About half of the west stand, including the dressing rooms, was burnt out before the fire was extinguished. The loss was serious owing to all the documents in the offices being destroyed. Initially the origin was unknown but it was thought to have been caused by a spark from one of the railway engines that ran on the westerly side of the ground. Another thought was that the fire originated from the heating apparatus. In the accounts for the season 1918/19 a sum of £560 was shown as being compensation for the damage.

MR CONSISTENCY

In September 1924 outside-left George Mee was presented with a gold watch by Blackpool supporters for a run of 162 consecutive appearances, which was extended to 194, [or 209, 219 or even 222 if some figures are to be accepted – the first mentioned figure, 209 (195 league and 14 FA Cup), seems to be the correct one although the Blackpool & Fylde Football Annual for 1926/27 stated, "George Mee made 194 consecutive appearances in the Blackpool League team, and 219 including Cup ties." Mee began his run on Christmas Day 1920 against Barnsley and it ended against Derby County on 12 September 1925, a most remarkable achievement. During the run Mee also played in 12 Lancashire Senior Cup ties.

UNSATISFACTORY OFFICIAL

At a meeting of the Blackpool directors on 16 October 1930 the secretary's request to forward a letter to the North West Mid-Week League Committee, copied to Burnley, was agreed. It was to complain of "the inefficiency of Mr Whitehead, the referee, in the Blackpool v Burnley match on 15 October asking him [sic] not to officiate again". Blackpool seemingly had grounds for complaint as they lost the game 7-2.

ROYAL BLUE

Blackpool introduced blue in their shirts and shorts for the opening league game of the 1983/84 season against the Royals of Reading. Manager Sam Ellis commented, "We have a shadow stripe in the shirt, which gives the strip a modern look. We've been trying to change the club's image all round, and a new-look strip is part of the new image. But we haven't gone too far from the traditional tangerine." The new image worked as Keith Mercer's goal gave Blackpool a 1-0 home win, the first of 21 victories that helped Blackpool to finish the season in sixth place in Division Four.

RICH PICKINGS

In the 1919/20 season Blackpool took £11,895 0s 4d in gate receipts, a club record up to that time, but the figure was bettered by almost every other First and Second Division club, only three being thought to have taken less.

GEORGE MEE, STANDING SECOND FROM RIGHT, WITH HIS TEAMMATES AT TRAINING IN THE MIDDLE OF HIS RECORD-BREAKING RUN OF CONSECUTIVE APPEARANCES.

SPECTATORS' WELFARE

In October 1976 Blackpool were planning to have automatic turnstiles installed at Bloomfield Road by Christmas 1976, "in readiness for life in the First Division", the latter an ambitious comment by the management. The automatic turnstiles would lead to greater efficiency and would make tallying of gate money much easier. The non-automatic turnstiles they would replace were fitted with a clock that registered the number of spectators passing through while the automatic ones would have a similar clock but the number of fans would be flashed through to a TV monitor in the secretary's office. The exact number would be recorded and as sections of the ground became full, the secretary would see on the monitor and switch fans to turnstiles where there was room in the ground. Secretary Des McBain said that the turnstiles were the most modern and sophisticated available and added, "ten years more advanced than Liverpool's. Nothing aggravates fans more than being kept hanging about in slow-moving queues, especially with kick-off time approaching. It is a worthwhile investment financially. We will save time and money."

DUCK A L'ORANGE!

In the late 1940s Sid Bevers of the Atomic Boys decided that a duck was to be the Blackpool mascot and the tradition lasted for a good number of years. However, Donald, named after the Walt Disney creation, the first of the duck mascots, died a violent death in an argument with a dog.

A GIANT OF THE GAME

When Blackpool entertained Barnsley at Raikes Hall on 15 March 1899 in a Second Division match, "the kick-off ceremony was performed by a giant, named Brough, said to be the tallest man on earth who stands seven feet five and a half inches." Despite his size and presence, "After he had set the ball rolling he dodged off the field in a wary manner, and only seemed safe when he got to his feet." He then watched Jack Parkinson open the scoring for Blackpool and an inside-forward called Gamble score two further goals to give Blackpool a 3-1 victory. Interestingly, Gamble played only five league games for Blackpool, in which he scored three goals, before disappearing from the first-class football scene.

MILITARY FOOTBALLERS

Blackpool was said to be fortunate to be able to draw on soldier footballers stationed in the town in the 1916/17 to 1918/19 seasons of World War I football. There was a Royal Army Medical Corps Depot at Squires Gate and also the King's Lancashire Military Convalescent Hospital and players were often recruited from both sources.

A NURSERY CLUB

History was almost repeating itself in the 1925/26 season when, 26 years after South Shore FC and Blackpool FC had amalgamated, the South Shore team that played in the West Lancashire League became a newly formed Blackpool 'A' team, a nursery in which Blackpool's junior players would be tried. The 'A' team was to be an independent section of the senior club and was to be governed by the officials of the old South Shore club, chairman Mr G Cowlishaw and vice-chairman Mr H 'Gyp' Cookson. The plan was that each week Blackpool would submit a list of their players who were not engaged and the Blackpool 'A' officials, ex-South Shore, would choose a team from those players. They would also consider any players who the senior club specially requested to be given a trial. The players would be allowed to train at Bloomfield Road, under expert supervision and, when it was possible, the Bloomfield Road ground would be used for West Lancashire League matches. The general view was "This is a great advance towards the complete co-operation between the senior club and the junior organisation in the town."

A RECORD CROWD

For the Good Friday Second Division game with Bury on 2 April 1920 Bloomfield Road had "never been so crowded" and a new record attendance was created. The capacity of the ground was stated to be 14,000 but there were 17,000 present and "The roofs of the stand were commandeered by spectators and on all sides the onlookers were wedged in like sardines and at places the barriers were broken down by the weight of the crowd." And "It was all they [the stewards] could do to keep people off the playing area." Most of the spectators went away happy because a solitary goal by Jack Charles won the game for Blackpool.

CROWD CONTROL

After the Chief Constable, Mr H Barnes, and the Borough Surveyor, Mr A S Hamilton, had spent an hour roaming around Bloomfield Road's Spion Kop on 10 April 1946, they decided that eight extra crush barriers had to be installed before the forthcoming Easter games. These were required to "prevent the possibility of any direct pressure down the terraces". It was also decided that the police would control the turnstiles for the last two home games so that they could, if necessary, close them down should they decide that enough spectators were already in the ground. As a result of the decision Blackpool decided to issue an extra 2,300 tickets at four shillings and sixpence for the games against Liverpool and Burnley. Chairman Colonel William Parkinson said, "We realised a year or two ago that it was no longer possible to accommodate a pre-war capacity attendance. We took all the necessary precautions to ensure that the attendances should always be limited to a thousand or two fewer than the new capacity figure. That policy we shall continue to pursue. There will be no endangering of the public safety on the Blackpool ground." Attendances had dropped since Blackpool's dismissal from the FA Cup with the average being around 10-12,000 but with the alterations the club were expecting nearer 20,000 for the final two games, this in spite of the fact that the West Stand entrances were all boarded up as the stand was closed. The press had been reallocated to the small stand in the south-west of the ground and the directors had been allocated an area in the centre of the South Stand but "providing labour and materials are released", the stand would be reopened for the 1946/47 season. Everything was in the event in vain for the attendances for the Liverpool and Burnley games were disappointing, 7,000 and 14,000 respectively. The Liverpool game was drawn 1-1 while Burnley were beaten 2-1 as Blackpool finished in a respectable ninth place in Division One.

A BAD IDEA

In November 1900 the Blackpool committee considered increasing the admission price for a forthcoming game against Burnley on 8 December from sixpence to one shilling [5p]. The *Gazette and News* commented, sarcastically, "Enterprising aren't they?" The committee eventually saw the error of their ways and stopped the idea, considering it "a thing repugnant"!

A YOUNGSTERS' STAND?

In late November 1933 there was a proposal put to the Blackpool directors by chairman Sir Lindsay Parkinson that a children's stand should be built at Bloomfield Road. This was "to encourage interest in league football for the youngsters of the town". Sir Lindsay had instigated a system whereby 1,000 tickets were distributed to the director of education for passing on to school children to attend Central League games. Nothing came of the proposal for the stand but even into the 1960s tickets for Central League games were given to schools for children to attend free of charge.

BLOOMFIELD SUPERSTORE

In March 1986 the Blackpool Football Club directors were ready to sell Bloomfield Road as a site for a superstore and a lucrative deal was being discussed with a Manchester development company. The directors wanted to either move to the nearby Blackpool Borough rugby league ground or to an alternative (unspecified) site where a superbowl stadium would be developed. Financial director Raschid Gibrail said, "The move would protect existing jobs at the soccer and rugby clubs and create new ones at the supermarket development, our new stadium and in the construction industry. It would also generate higher rate revenue for the Town Hall and we would bring money-spinning events to our new stadium, which would keep money in the town and boost the local economy." However, Blackpool fans did not want to leave Bloomfield Road and voiced their opinions and in the end nothing came of the proposal.

MATCH COMFORT

There were cushions for hire at the home game against Preston North End on 28 August 1933 as the new board of directors had sanctioned a proposal submitted on behalf of the supporters' club by Mr W S Lines to supply cushions to spectators. There was only a limited number available for the first week, 150 to 200, but if demand warranted it, several thousand were to be purchased. The cushions were rented for 2d (1p) each or five shillings (25p) for the whole season. The trial was a success and there were 2-3,000 available by the end of September 1933 and public demand increased accordingly.

HORSE PLAY

Prior to the opening home league game of the season on 5 September 1921, the horse roller had rolled the pitch at Bloomfield Road in the morning and the ground was said to have "looked at its best". Blackpool certainly weren't at their best as they lost 1-0 to Bury.

TEA TOTALLERS!

Manager Allan Brown, determined to get the club out of the Fourth Division, put a drinks curfew on his players in August 1981 as he did not want the squad wrecked by ill discipline. Any player caught drinking within two days of a game was to be severely dealt with as Brown commented, "A couple of drinks never harmed any player … you can sweat it out. But you can't put back lost sleep. We have to have discipline. You need it in any job especially professional football. We have to convince our players that they are athletes and athletes do not run themselves down with excessive drinks and late nights." He added that he did not anticipate any problems because "I believe we have gathered a good bunch of professionals and I think they will respond well because they have the right character."

YOUNGEST EVER

Eamonn Collins became Blackpool's youngest ever first-team player when he went on as a 78th-minute substitute in the Anglo-Scottish Cup game against Kilmarnock on 9 September 1980. He was 14 years and 324 days old when he played his part in Blackpool's 2-1 victory. He commented on his debut, "The crowd kept chanting my name and I had a great chance of scoring, but it just missed the post."

BARREN SPELL

Blackpool defeated Chesterfield Town 1-0 away on 2 March 1907 with an own goal by a Chesterfield defender but then they embarked on a disastrous run away from home that saw them play 41 games before the next victory. They drew 11 games and lost 30 over a period of 30 months before defeating Manchester City 2-1 with goals from George Beare and Harry Dawson in the opening game of the 1909/10 season on 2 September 1909.

HAVE BOOTS - CAN'T TRAVEL

The Government imposed a travel ban on 1 April 1942 and Blackpool had to pull out of the Wartime Cup (North) as players were not allowed to leave the town where they were garrisoned. This meant that Blackpool only had one player, Alex Roxburgh, stationed in the auxiliary fire service in Manchester, who could play in the match against Manchester City on 6 April 1942. Ten of the usual 11 would be absent so Colonel W Parkinson, the Blackpool chairman, announced, "I think our only course is to resign from the cup. Probably from somewhere, or other, in the Fylde we could unearth ten young players, but it would be an insult to the city to send such a team to Maine Road, and it would make Blackpool look ridiculous." Manchester City had 75% of their side stationed in Manchester so they would have been able to raise a fairly representative side. The Blackpool chairman sent a telegram to Capt H H Balfour, the Parliamentary under secretary for air, protesting that the ban was in direct conflict with the Government's decree permitting professional football during the weekend. The telegram stated, "Nearly every club in the cup will be affected. The ban merely penalises those clubs which have been patriotic, and where players have entered the services." The chairman also said, "Unless the ban is lifted Blackpool will be out of the cup. We cannot field a team against Manchester City either on Saturday or Monday in present circumstances. Only a goalkeeper is left. As 46 of Blackpool's 48 registered players are in the services, the ban merely means that a team that has realised its obligations to the country and nearly all of whose players have gone into the fighting forces cannot even play in the cup, whereas a club where players, although of military age, have remained in civilian occupations can not only play in it but win it." The Government replied to the Blackpool chairman with "Ministry regrets that no relaxation of the ban is justified." Even though Manchester City were prepared to compromise with a midweek game at Blackpool there would have been a problem with a second leg so Colonel Parkinson finally said, "That's settled it. We regret Blackpool's decision but we agree it was unavoidable. The club were given too short notice of the ban. There was no time to select an alternative team, even the if the material had been available." The cup favourites were out of the competition.

IN FOR A PENNY

There was a deputation from the Blackpool Supporters' Club, consisting of Messrs Handel Wilde, Dubbin and Lines, which met the directors in September 1930 to express concern about the dropping of their Penny on the Ball moneymaking scheme. They felt that it brought them into closer contact with supporters and that because the club was in the First Division the increased number of spectators would put more money into the club's coffers. The plea was in vain for at a subsequent meeting of the directors on 19 September 1930 "It was unanimously resolved to adhere to our previous decision and the Secretary [was] requested to notify them to this effect."

NO MONEY SPINNER

When Old Corinthians came to play an exhibition game against Blackpool on 9 April 1885 they were said to be "high among the first rank on present day football circles". The Blackpool committee therefore thought that the game would be a money-spinner but just in case it proved not to be, some guarantors were procured to make good any loss on the day. Blackpool lost the game 2-1 and the promoters were considerably the losers as it was reported, "Blackpool people, in the bulk, do not seem to possess much of the footballing spirit" as gate receipts totalled just £12. The club had to meet half the expenses incurred, a loss was in the offing and, therefore, the unfortunate guarantors were called in.

NIGHT OWLS

When the ground staff arrived at Bloomfield Road early on 18 April 1964 they discovered that during the night intruders had broken in and painted the south end goalposts blue. And on the wall fronting the barriers near the goal was painted 'Up the Owls'. "We could only assume," said Blackpool secretary Fred Jones, "that some time during the night Sheffield Wednesday fans broke into the ground. By an unfortunate mischance the night watchman had been taken ill and had been compelled to go home, leaving the ground unattended." Ground staff spent a couple of hours cleaning up and removing the paint and when the game kicked off there was no trace of any graffiti. The game was drawn 2-2 with Blackpool's goals coming from John McPhee and Des Horne.

LIKE FATHER LIKE SON

Michael Docherty, son of Tommy Docherty, joined Blackpool's backroom staff in January 1988 on trial and signed a two-year deal with the club in May 1988. He left Blackpool, where he had been reserve team coach, to become assistant at Burnley under Frank Casper in January 1989. Blackpool boss Sam Ellis said, "Mick has done a smashing job for us in the time he has been at Blackpool. It is a good move for him and in fact Frank Casper has been interested in taking Mick as his assistant since the day he took over at Burnley a couple of weeks ago. Mick follows Bobby Downes, Bob Ward and Bob Saxton to other jobs and it says a lot for the calibre of people we have at the club. I wish Mick all the best in his new role. There are no plans at the moment to appoint a replacement for Mick. It is time for all of us at the club to pull together and get on with the job we need to do. Jimmy Mullen will be in charge of the reserve team at Port Vale on Wednesday." Docherty commented, "I wouldn't have left Sam Ellis for anything else, and I will always be grateful to him for bringing me back into football again and giving me a chance after two years away from the game. But when Frank Casper contacted me it was too good an opportunity to miss and I am looking forward to starting work." Casper said, "We have a long, hard job to do at Burnley and we need to do it properly. That's why I have brought in a man like Mick. He is a very good coach and a disciplinarian, and we have known each other a long time."

FOGGED OFF

In an English Cup third qualifying round replay at Bloomfield Road on 6 November 1901, Blackpool of Division Two had drawn 0-0 with Southport Central of the Lancashire League when the final whistle went. The referee ordered extra-time to be played but "the mist which had cleared off to enable the match to be played, now appeared again and after eight minutes of extra-time, the referee blew his whistle" and the game was abandoned. The draw for the fourth qualifying round took place and paired the winners of the tie with Workington but in the second replay at Deepdale, Blackpool lost 2-1 with 'Geordie' Anderson scoring Blackpool's goal. Ironically ten days later Blackpool had another game fogged off at Bloomfield Road, this time before half-time. They were losing 1-0 to Leicester Fosse on 16 November 1901 and when it was replayed on 15 March 1902, Blackpool lost 1-0.

TRAINING EMBARGO

The *Daily Mail* of Wednesday, 16 November 1977 carried a story that Blackpool players had refused to train on the Tuesday of that week unless they were taken to the Squires Gate training ground by bus. The players denied this to be the case although they did admit that they were fighting for better changing conditions at the training ground. They had refused to get changed at Squires Gate as they considered the facilities to be poor and they had been going to Bloomfield Road to change prior to going to the training ground. The club at first laid on a coach costing £50 per week to ferry them back and forth but the bus was then stopped and the 'A' team minibus was used. It had broken down on the Tuesday in question; manager Allan Brown commented, "Exhaust fumes were belching out and it was not at all pleasant." He originally wanted the players to run to Squires Gate along the road or on the beach but he eventually decided against it because of gale-force winds! The senior players assured everyone that there was no question of a revolt! However the training protest was still ongoing in December when the players refused to change at Squires Gate until the floors were improved and a bath was provided.

MONEY TROUBLES

The *Pall Mall Gazette* reported on 27 October 1898, "Blackpool Football Club issued an appeal yesterday for immediate support in consequence of financial predicament. If funds are not forthcoming the club will have to wind up, and earn the unenviable distinction of being the only League club that has failed to complete its engagements. The players have agreed to wait a week for their salaries. A committee has been formed to stave off disaster."

EUELL DO

Jason Euell's goal that defeated Ipswich Town on 6 March 2010 gave Blackpool their first league win over the East Anglian side since 20 August 1962 when a Des Horne goal gave Blackpool a 1-0 victory. Euell's goal ended a run of 12 games against Ipswich without a victory and it was only the sixth goal Blackpool had scored at home against Ipswich in eight league games since the rivalry began on 28 October 1961.

EARLY KICK-OFF

As part of the plan to save fuel and cut back on costly electricity with the use of the floodlights in late 1979 Blackpool changed the time of their home Central League kick-offs to 2pm on a Saturday for the months of November and December 1979 and January 1980. The new policy began with the game against Burnley reserves on 3 November 1979 and "Inevitably there was some effect on the size of the crowd at the start." A goal from Wayne Harrison won the game for Blackpool.

A CHARITY INTERNATIONAL

An England versus Scotland game was played at Bloomfield Road on 2 January 1918 when the two teams, representative of the two nations, were composed of members of the Royal Army Medical Corps that was based in Blackpool. England fielded Monaghan, Bates, Moulson, Edge, Kinsella, Grice, Southern, Moorcroft, Ralphs, Eccleston and Stimson. Scotland fielded Sperrin, Fairhurst, Hankin, Hannay, Prosser, Bradley, Elliott, Robb, Bold, Fraser and McCready. The game ended in a 1-1 draw with the goals coming from Moorcroft for England and Prosser for Scotland. A crowd of 5,000 watched with the proceeds going to the children of soldiers blinded during the war. There had been a previous game on 14 November 1917 when England had defeated Scotland 3-2.

NO LISBON LION FOR BLACKPOOL

In January 1960 a 16-year-old Scotsman, Bobby Lennox, who was a milk delivery boy in his home town of Saltcoats, was brought to Bloomfield Road for trials after manager Ronnie Suart thought that his future lay in football not milk delivering. He spent a month or so at Bloomfield Road where he played in the junior sides but was then allowed to return home as Blackpool did not wish to take up their option on him. He returned to Scottish junior football with Ardeer Recreation and then in 1961 Glasgow Celtic signed him and he went on to score 273 goals for the club and was one of the 'Lisbon Lions' who defeated Inter Milan 2-1 in the 1967 European Cup Final. He also won ten Scottish international caps and was inducted into the Scottish Football Hall of Fame in 2005 – a case of very much 'almost' for Blackpool!

RAIN PROTECTION

On 27 July 1937 it was announced that Blackpool Football Club were considering covering the Spion Kop to at least three-quarters of the way up the terracing. Such a roof would be extended to the Supporters' Club Stand, the east paddock, thus bridging the gap at the north-east corner of the ground. In addition there would be central turnstiles on the east side to ease the pressure on Bloomfield Road and its approaches. The covering of the Kop was subsequently left in abeyance for some 20 years.

THE LUCK OF THE IRISH

An Irish Alliance side played a Blackpool side of reserve and irregular players at Bloomfield Road on Good Friday 13 April 1909 and the Blackpool directors hoped that it would prove an attractive fixture. It did not, there were "very few in" and the game was a financial disaster and Blackpool also lost 4-2 with goals from Gillibrand, who also broke his arm, and Slade.

A GOOD READ

For the game against Cardiff City on 4 October 1969 Blackpool printed 7,000 programmes, which was deemed sufficient for an anticipated crowd of 21,000. The programme sold out even though the crowd was only 18,115 and secretary Des McBain commented, "One chap took a bundle under each arm and put them in his car. There must have been at least 100. We've never seen supporters buying programmes in such numbers."

FEET FIRST

Blackpool became the first club in the game's history to appoint a full-time chiropodist. It was not uncommon for league clubs to have an honorary chiropodist but Blackpool's appointment was the first time one had been on the list of permanent officials at a league club. Mr G Entwistle, once of the London Foot Hospital, was appointed on 21 August 1939 and he was to be in attendance at the ground every Monday morning and in addition the club would be able to call him in for a consultation or for treatment at any other time. The press comment was an amusing "Feet are important in football. Blackpool are apparently one of the first clubs to appreciate the fact."

CHARITY CUP

In April 1925 the directors of Blackpool's Savoy Café donated a handsome silver challenge cup to Blackpool for them to play another league team in a one-off cup match at the end of each season. The opposition would be by invite only and proceeds from each game would be given to Blackpool Victoria Hospital. Everton were the first opponents in the Victoria Hospital Cup competition on 9 May 1925 and with Blackpool having finished the 1924/25 season in a disappointing 17th place in Division Two and Everton having been in a similar position but in Division One, the Toffees were favourites to win. Blackpool fielded two trialists in Jarrett and Mercer in a line-up that was Crompton, Wood, Jones, Mercer, Jarrett, Benton, Meredith, Watson, Bedford, Butler and Mee. Harry Bedford and Herbert Butler gave Blackpool a two-goal advantage at half-time and even though Chedgzoy pulled one back for Everton in the second half, Blackpool held on to win 2-1. Mr John Hacking, chairman of the directors of the Savoy Café, presented the cup to Blackpool captain Billy Benton and at the same time he very cordially thanked all the players for their gratuitous services. Raising the cup, Benton replied with a smile, "We only wish it had been the English Cup." There was to be a wait of another 28 years before that feat was accomplished.

BEST SINCE MATTHEWS

Speaking of his appointment of Alan Ball as manager in February 1980, Blackpool chairman Peter Lawson commented, "I believe we are making the most forward step that a board has ever made since the days when Blackpool signed Stanley Matthews."

CHINESE TAKEAWAY

In a Central League game on 19 August 1961 Cheung Chi Doy scored three goals in capital style for Blackpool reserves with John Craven and Graham Oates scoring the other two in a 5-0 thrashing of Barnsley reserves.

LANDMARK GOAL

Keith Southern scored Blackpool's 6,000th goal in league football: the only goal of the game in the 1-0 win over Leicester City on 11 August 2007.

INVALUABLE ASSISTANCE

The Blackpool Football Club Supporters' Club was formed in January 1925 when there was a financial crisis at the parent club. The football club had a general meeting in the Free Library to explain the position and immediately afterwards those interested in forming a supporters' club met and 200 to 300 members were immediately registered. Mr Handel Wilde was appointed chairman and following meetings held at the Tower Circus, Winter Gardens and at St Annes there was a membership of 1,500 within a few weeks. This number rose to 2,500 by the start of the 1926/27 season. The committee worked with enthusiasm to raise money for the benefit of the football club and very soon the crisis at the club was over. Thereafter the supporters' club considered the best means of using other money they raised and it was decided to erect a stand on the popular (east) side of the ground. A ladies' committee was also formed, under the leadership of Miss L Furber, and many social events were held to augment funds. In March 1926 a contract was signed for the erection of the new east stand at a total cost of £2,500. In addition to raising money for the club, members of the supporters' club committee sold over £700 worth of season tickets and a large number of shares were taken up by members. The new stand, with £700 having been spent on steel work, was partly ready for the 1926/27 season and it was the committee's intention to eventually cover the whole of the east side with a stand.

GOOD TRAVELLERS

In the ill-fated First Division relegation season of 1966/67, Blackpool gained more points away from Bloomfield Road than they did at it. Only seven points were gained at home with only one victory, 6-0 over Newcastle United, and five draws, 1-1 against Leicester City, Sheffield Wednesday, Sunderland and Nottingham Forest and 2-2 against Tottenham Hotspur. Fourteen points were won away from home with wins at Tottenham, 3-1, Everton, 1-0, Southampton 5-1, Chelsea 2-0 and Liverpool 3-1, and draws at Arsenal, Sheffield United and Leeds United, all 1-1, and at Fulham, 2-2. Indeed, Blackpool won more games on Merseyside, two, than they did all season at home, one, and the six points earned in London very nearly equalled the overall total gained at home!

ON AIR

At a directors' meeting on 1 October 1930 Dr Simpson and Mr Howcroft met the Blackpool board and asked if the club were prepared to allow their firm to install Radio Recordian plant on the ground. They were prepared to pay ten shillings (50p) per thousand spectators attending the match and would also give out half-time scores and a musical programme. After a long discussion it was agreed to leave the matter in the hands of two of the directors, Messrs Hindley and Hargreaves. An agreement was obviously reached because at the directors' meeting on 9 October 1930 it was reported that Mr Butterworth had visited the Newcastle United ground and seen the Radio Recordian installation there and he was "much impressed". As such he stated that the club had done well in signing the agreement.

HE'S IN CHARGE

Blackpool's first official team manager was Bill Norman, who was appointed at the club's annual general meeting on 19 May 1919. He remained in the post until 1923 when he moved to Leeds United as assistant manager. Prior to Norman, although Blackpool did not officially have a manager, Jack Cox, who was re-signed on a free transfer from Liverpool on 16 August 1909, was unofficially known as 'player-manager'. Cox had originally been with Blackpool in the 1897/98 season before moving to Liverpool and in his second spell with Blackpool he remained for three seasons. After retirement he became a noted crown greens bowls player.

CHANGE OF VENUE

Blackpool's Lancashire League clash with local rivals South Shore had to be moved from Blackpool's Raikes Hall Gardens ground, where a health exhibition was being staged, to South Shore's Waterloo Road ground and the move favoured South Shore for they won 1-0. As a consequence the return game was rescheduled for Raikes Hall and was played on 9 December 1899. The crowd was Blackpool's largest of the season and an own goal and one from Johnson gave Blackpool a 2-1 victory and left them in fifth place in the table with South Shore ninth. At the conclusion of the game little did anyone realise that it was the quietus for South Shore as that same evening the club folded and amalgamated with Blackpool.

BREAKING THE 20,000 BARRIER

Good Friday, 18 April 1930, was the first time that Bloomfield Road housed more than 20,000 spectators for a league match. Thousands stormed the ground and a few of the gates crumpled under the avalanche of people. When it had all been sorted out the box office reported that 23,868 spectators had paid then record receipts of £1,825 14s 3d to see a game that for all intents and purposes decided the Second Division promotion race. With goals from Jack Oxberry, Jimmy Hampson and 'Jazz' Rattray, Blackpool defeated Oldham Athletic 3-0 and more or less made certain of their championship aspirations, which were to come to fruition the following month.

NO PORTUGUESE MAN O' WAR

Jose Antonio Nunes was a Portuguese midfield player who Blackpool were prepared to consider signing in late October 1979. The 23-year-old was with the Portuguese First Division side Estoril although he was studying and had not played for the club for five months. As such, it was possible that he would be available on a free transfer with the Blackpool connection having arisen because he had had a holiday romance with a Blackpool girl. There was a problem in that the question of a work permit had to be sorted out should manager Stan Ternent receive confirmation that no fee for the player was involved. In mid-November Nunes sent a photograph to the club and stated that he definitely wanted to join Blackpool because he was marrying a local girl. International clearance was required and Blackpool were still concerned about getting him a work permit. In addition chief scout Peter Doherty was hoping that the player would come over for a holiday so that he could have a look at him. When he sent the photograph he had added another name so was then known as Antonio Jose Nunes Martins! Perhaps not surprisingly in the circumstances, Nunes did not join Blackpool.

THE WRONG CAR

In 1971 goalkeeper John 'Budgie' Burridge treated himself to a new car, a Lotus Europa. When manager Bob Stokoe saw it he ordered Burridge to sell it immediately as he felt that it wasn't a good image for a 19-year-old footballer! Burridge duly did so and bought a Triumph Spitfire instead.

IN OR OUT?

Oval goalposts were introduced for the 1925/26 season instead of the usual square woodwork and there was much speculation about their usefulness. The argument was that when the ball hit the square woodwork, particularly the crossbar, and bounced towards the line, unless the referee were close at hand to see whether the ball had crossed the line, there was heated debates amongst the spectators (and presumably the players) about whether a goal had been scored or not. With oval woodwork, expectations were that the ball would bounce into the goal more definitely. Blackpool first used the oval goalposts in the pre-season practice games of that season and two shots hit the woodwork and while square woodwork might have led to confusion, the oval equivalent allowed one shot to turn into the goal and the other to deflect over the bar. One sceptic said, tongue in cheek, after the games "Elastic goalposts might be better." Their usefulness was demonstrated for the first time in a league game at Bloomfield Road against Derby County on 12 September 1925. An oblique shot from Derby outside -left Murphy struck the far post, but instead of rebounding onto the goal line or into the net, as it might have done with a square post, the ball was a yard or more clear of the line when it reached the ground. This seemed to obviate any arguments as to where the ball landed but Blackpool still lost the game 2-1.

FIGHTING TALK

Bob Brocklebank, manager of Second Division Birmingham City, said confidently before the FA Cup semi-final on 11 March 1951, "My boys are cup conscious this year, and so far they have always been able to pull out that little bit extra in the cup ties. I know that Blackpool are a stiff obstacle, but we had obstacles in Derby County and Manchester United, and we came through. It is a good draw and if the lads play as well as they did in the last round against Manchester United we shall give Blackpool a good game, if we do not beat them." Blackpool were seventh in Division One while Birmingham were sixth in Division Two but despite this disparity the first meeting at Maine Road was drawn 0-0. In the replay at Goodison Park, goals from Stan Mortensen and Bill Perry put Blackpool through to Wembley 2-1.

THE BATTLE OF HASTINGS

When Blackpool played Hastings & St Leonards in the first round of the FA Cup at Bloomfield Road on 16 January 1909, a large crowd was not expected because of the quality of the opposition. The tie attracted the smallest attendance of the first round, 2,765. Blackpool, who played in the reserve side's light and dark blue kit to avoid clashing with the strawberry colours of the visitors, won 2-0 with goals from Arthur Whalley and Ted Threlfall but the gate receipts were only £81 and "after deducting the expenses of the match, [they were] not sufficient for each club to pay the week's expenses".

NOT AULD TIME

Blackpool had agreed a £15,000 transfer fee with Glasgow Celtic for Scottish international winger Bertie Auld in January 1961 when the club were looking for a replacement for the injury-hit Bill Perry. However the deal fell through at the last minute when Auld had a financial disagreement with Celtic and Blackpool were "bitterly disappointed". Auld eventually joined Birmingham City in May 1951.

HOME FROM HOME

When Blackpool went into special training for their first round FA Cup tie against Derby County, scheduled for Bloomfield Road on 10 January 1920, they chose Blackpool's Balmoral Hotel on South Promenade as their base. Fourteen players were based at the hotel for the week prior to the game and "healthy pedestrian exercise" was undertaken. A walk from Lytham to Blackpool on Tuesday morning was followed by a walk from Cleveleys to Blackpool on Wednesday afternoon. In between, ball practice at Bloomfield Road was the order of the day. The game was drawn 0-0 but two goals from Joe Lane and one each from Jack Charles and Jack Sibbald gave the Seasiders a 4-1 victory in the replay. Buoyed by the experience, and the victory, Blackpool returned to the Balmoral prior to the second round tie against Preston North End at Deepdale. Once again there was "a quick walk on the promenade" to ensure "the requisite amount of walking" was done and ball practice again took place at Bloomfield Road. But this time the ploy did not work because a Peter Quinn goal was all Blackpool could offer in reply to Preston's two goals.

ADMINISTRATIVE ERROR

The Football League announced on 17 January 1983 that Blackpool were to be deducted two points for fielding an ineligible player earlier in the 1982/83 season. It transpired that it was John Butler and that he had played three games, two in the league and one League Cup tie, before his registration had been confirmed. Blackpool explained that they had signed him as a professional on 8 September 1982 and had immediately sent off his registration forms to the Football League, who were then located at nearby Lytham St Annes. The reason that the forms were posted was that there was no urgency in getting him registered as he was not in the immediate first-team plans. However a spate of injuries in the week before the Bristol City game on 11 September 1982 meant that he was selected and played in a 0-0 draw. The League said that they had no doubt that Blackpool had posted the relevant forms but explained that Blackpool should have received confirmation of his registration and having received no such confirmation they should have contacted the Football League at once and not simply played Butler. Not having done so meant that Butler was ineligible to play. Dick Wragg headed a Football League Management Committee tribunal that investigated the matter on 13 January 1983 and decided on the punishment of a two-point deduction. Blackpool decided not to appeal against the penalty as there were stiffer options available to the committee, such as a three-point deduction and a stiff fine. Meanwhile the assistant head postmaster at Blackpool, Mr Cliff Ratcliffe, commented, "The extent of this problem has now been drawn to my attention so I am having a further look at this and getting more people involved in the investigation. It is a strange case, quite baffling. Only outgoing mail is involved and no other local firm has informed us of a similar problem." Blackpool did not agree and commented that a recent incoming letter to the club, ironically from the Post Office, had also gone astray.

A FIVE-FIGURE CROWD

Blackpool's first 10,000 crowd at Bloomfield Road was against Oldham Athletic on 12 September 1908 when a goal from Billy Weston won the game 1-0 for the Seasiders. There was not to be another such crowd until Burnley visited on 25 March 1910.

RISING COSTS

At Blackpool's annual general meeting on 29 June 1891 it was noted that the players' wage bill for the 1890/91 season was £379 14s 4d out of a total expenditure of £823 19s 9d, the second largest item of expenditure being the travelling expenses at £139 8s 2d. The wage bill compared favourably to those such as Notts County, £1,996, Blackburn Rovers, £1,324, and Nottingham Forest, £1,289 but even so the club made a loss of just over £30 on the season as income totalled only £793 2s 5d with gate receipts at £326 15s 2d plus stand receipts of £110 17s 0d being the two main contributors. There were complaints about the extra money charged for stand tickets but it was agreed that such arrangements would continue in an effort to keep the club solvent.

GLORIOUS GUNNERS

In three successive seasons Arsenal created a new attendance record at Bloomfield Road. In 1930 in Blackpool's first game in the First Division there were 27,694 present, in 1931 the attendance was 29,439 and in 1932 it was 30,265. Blackpool lost all three games, 4-1 on 30 August 1930, 5-1 on 10 October 1931 and 2-1 on 1 October 1932. The first game also produced record gate receipts of £1,886 2s 6d.

PRIVATE FRIENDLY

In a behind-closed-doors friendly game against York City on 26 February 1980 Blackpool came from behind to win 2-1 with goals from Max Thompson and Jimmy Weston.

REMOTE CHANGING

For the pre-season practice game played at Bloomfield Road on 25 August 1900, the players had to change at the nearby Bridge House Hotel because no changing facilities were then available at the new ground. Changing tents were provided for the opening league game against Gainsborough Trinity on 8 September when a Bob Birket goal earned Blackpool a point in a 1-1 draw. However, it was the only league game of the 1900/01 season that was played at Bloomfield Road for the club returned to their more central Raikes Hall Gardens ground for the remainder of the season.

THE EXOTIC MIDDLE EAST

Blackpool Football Club went on a brief three-day visit to Saudi Arabia in November 1976 and it was considered by the players to be "quite an experience, but one that wouldn't need repeating too often". The flight out was by TriStar, paid for at "over £400 per head" by the hosts, and the hospitality was, as was to be expected in the wealthy Arab state, first-class within their people's way of life. The trip cost the Saudi magnates many thousands of pounds but they felt that it was money well spent. The players considered the living conditions to be "tough", they considered the food "wasn't too clever", several meals being taken at the American steak bars, and they did not sleep too well for they were regularly awakened when locals were called to prayer at 4.30 every morning. And finally the return journey was a 21-hour flight, which left the players absolutely shattered. Senior director Stan Parr, who was familiar with that part of the world having served in the forces in the Middle East from 1948 to 1950, said that apart from the superb football stadium that sprang up from the desert like a mirage, the Saudis had advanced much in terms of facilities since his days there. He added, "They have a leisurely way of life and like to go very much at their own pace." One offshoot from the visit was expected to be reciprocal visits by Saudi teams to Blackpool. One of the biggest successes of the trip was the final day when the Blackpool party was invited to spend it at the British Embassy and was able to use the swimming pool, squash courts and other sports facilities. The stadium where the game was played held 50,000 of which 40,000 were seated and Blackpool won the game 5-0 against a Bill McGarry-managed Saudi Arabia national side that treated it as a warm-up game for their World Cup qualifier against Syria. Blackpool attracted a crowd of 25,000 and earned an estimated £18,000 from the trip, considerably more than was at first thought. Full-back Steve Harrison, who had built up quite a reputation for his mimicry and leg-pulling, was the life and soul of the party with his impersonations of coach Stewart Imlach often bringing the house down, as did his impersonation of Frank Spencer (nothing changes for Steve is still a very funny man today). The players' overall view of Saudi Arabia was that it was "a place that must grow on you".

A SPORTS CENTRE OF THE NORTH

In late October 1938 the possibility of a super stadium replacing Blackpool's Bloomfield Road ground was not just a dream as it was seriously under review in municipal circles. The plan was for "every branch of modern sport and physical culture" to be accommodated within the stadium with football in the winter and other "sports events and displays" in the summer. The estimated cost of the stadium was £150,000 and, if developed, it was to be an all-seater stadium accommodating 80,000 spectators. Blackpool Football Club would put up £100,000 at three per cent interest and Blackpool Corporation would put up the other £50,000 on similar terms. The proposal was that Blackpool Football Club would hand over Bloomfield Road and the Corporation would enlarge it by including land on the east side up to Henry Street and they would also secure 50 feet of land over the railway sidings on the west side. A Corporation spokesman said, "Such a stadium is a practical proposition. It would be another permanent attraction for Blackpool, and we cannot have too many of those. The stadium would be a place fit for any national sporting event, and it will have to receive consideration as a suitable venue for semi-finals in the cup ties." Another advocate of the scheme added, "If we have the modern stadium, Blackpool may once again be able to get in on the ground floor in a movement of national interest, and become the great sports and health centre of the north, or even of the whole of England, for we have the additional asset of the sea breezes. The football ground is an ideal site for the stadium. It will be near to the new Central Station, and there is a capacious car park adjoining it. We could not have anything better." Be that as it may, nothing came of the scheme.

RINGING THE CHANGES

By the time Blackpool played Reading on 10 November 1928 the club had used 23 players and made 31 changes in just 14 games. Only one player, Albert Watson, had played all the games in the same position while Jimmy Hampson had missed only one game. However, the changes for the Reading game were very successful for Blackpool won 7-0, Hampson scoring five, and Oxberry, two.

BAD LIGHT

The opening game of the 1907/08 season against Stockport County on 2 September 1907 ended in controversy because "The kick-off was arranged too late for the game to be finished in a proper light and it was owing to the darkness that Tillotson was defeated in the last two minutes of the match, which ensured the result to be a draw." Bob Whittingham had given Blackpool the lead but the late goal, in near darkness, gave Stockport a share of the points with a 1-1 draw. By the time of the equaliser, many of the spectators had left the ground satisfied that the home side had lost 1-0 with the Seasiders having "gained a creditable victory"!

GIVE YOUNGSTERS A CHANCE

Blackpool Football Club, along with a number of other Lancashire clubs, started a third team, named Blackpool 'A', to "give youngsters a chance" in 1922. The first game for Blackpool 'A' was against Burnley 'A' on Wednesday 22 February 1922 when Blackpool with a consolation goal from Alvey lost 3-1. The Blackpool team that contested that first game was Hacking, Jenkinson (a trialist from Oswaldtwistle), Johnson, Ferry, Cookson, Baker L H, Gilpin, Roberts, Alvey, Milner and Marr. Only Jack Hacking and Len Baker went on to appear in Blackpool's league side and goalkeeper Hacking, who was given a free transfer after playing 33 games over a three-season spell, later won three England caps when with Oldham Athletic in 1928/29.

A NEW GROUND

It was announced at the Blackpool Cricket and Football Club annual tea party, concert and ball held at the Assembly Rooms, Talbot Road on 11 December 1884 by Mr W C Thompson in his vote of thanks that the football side of the club "had taken a suitable ground in Raikes Hall Gardens, where they intended shortly to erect a grandstand and other necessary conveniences". The opening game on the new ground was against Fleetwood Rangers on 20 December 1884 but, sadly, only 200 spectators attended to see Blackpool lose 2-1.

SHORTEST

Blackpool wing-half Syd Tufnell at five foot two and three-quarter inches tall is reputedly the shortest wing-half ever to have played league football. Tufnell joined the Seasiders in May 1927 from Worksop Town and despite his size he was known as "a really big man in the tackle". He played 99 league and cup games, scoring four goals, and 149 Central League games, scoring nine goals before Blackpool transferred him to Wigan Athletic for a fee of £250 in August 1934.

THIRTEEN-A-SIDE

Bloomfield Road played host to rugby league for the first time on 5 September 1923 when Leeds played Barrow in a friendly game with Leeds winning 37-27. It was an attempt to encourage the growth of the game in Blackpool but, even though there were a few thousand curious spectators present, the game did not catch on in the town for a further 30 years.

A CHAMPION GOALKEEPER

Blackpool's only world champion was goalkeeper Tommy Wilcox, who from the age of 17, lived in America and while there he won the World Punchball Championship, a sport with boxing tendencies that was centred around a punchball that had gymnastic routines associated with it. He returned to England at the turn of the 19th century and after playing for Millwall Athletic, Cray Wanderers, Woolwich Arsenal and Norwich City, he signed for Blackpool on 30 May 1906.

IDENTIFIED FLYING OBJECTS

On Boxing Day 1935 Mr A Taylor, the referee in the Blackpool versus Burnley game at Bloomfield Road, reported to the Football Association that an orange and a walnut had been thrown at the Burnley goalkeeper, Robert Scott, by the Blackpool fans. The FA Emergency Committee considered the referee's report and decided to take no further action.

SYD TUFNELL WEIGHS IN PRESEASON WATCHED BY TRAINER ALLAN URE AND ALBERT WATSON.

BRACING SEA BREEZES!

When Blackpool played Newcastle United at St James' Park in the English Cup third round on 24 February 1906, Blackpool seized the opportunity to advertise the town "as a seaside and health resort" in the streets of Newcastle before the game. Twenty sheet pictorial posters of the town, 30 sheet posters of the tower, 50 advertising sandwich-board men and two special advertising carts in front of the station were used and hundreds of holiday guides were distributed about the city. In addition, every seat in the grandstand had a booklet about Blackpool placed on it and Alderman Tom Bickerstaffe and Councillor Parkinson, the town's representatives, were delighted with the efforts. "Spend your holidays at Blackpool, the unrivalled seaside resort for health and pleasure" was the message being put across. Charles Norden, the town's advertising manager, was most impressed with the efforts of the football club and commented, "We would have bought the blooming ground if they had let us have it." The local press felt that the value of the football club was "never better exemplified". The venture was repeated to a degree when Blackpool played Newcastle United at St James' Park in the English [FA] Cup second round on 6 February 1909, when Charles Norden, taking his lead from the previous occasion, arranged for 100 men with advertising sandwich boards, three or four lorries and the Blackpool Lifeboat Band to parade around the streets of Newcastle before the game to advertise Blackpool's claims as the country's leading health resort. It might have encouraged people to visit Blackpool but neither campaign did the football club much good for they lost both games, 5-0 in 1906 and 2-1 in 1909.

ALLITERATION

After Blackpool defeated Heywood Central 3-1 in a Lancashire League game on 18 February 1893, a Heywood mill-hand said, "Blackpool should add B.B.B.B.B.B.B. to their title." When asked why, he replied that he thought Blackpool were the best blooming bouncers ever beaten by Bury, the league leaders who had beaten Blackpool 4-0 a month earlier!

LET THERE BE LIGHT

The Bloomfield Road floodlights were reduced in size in 1990 as the larger variety, which were installed in the summer of 1958, were deemed unsafe.

GOLDEN GOALLESS

When John Burridge kept a clean sheet against West Bromwich Albion on 31 March 1975 he broke George Farm's long-standing record of 19 clean sheets in a season with a 20th game without conceding a goal. Regular ball sponsor Mr R Wintrip of Thornton presented him with the match ball after the game. Burridge kept one further clean sheet before the season ended, extending his new record to 21 games, before conceding seven goals in the final two games, 3-0 and 4-0 defeats by Aston Villa and Manchester United respectively. Chairman Frank Dickinson later presented Burridge with an inscribed clock from the directors commemorating his feat and manager Harry Potts commented, "Well done to John who has so dedicated himself to the game and is so worthy of his achievement."

UNLUCKY UDO

Hammersmith–born Udo Onwere was signed by Blackpool from Dover Athletic in September 1996 after having spells in the league with Fulham and Lincoln City. In all he made 27 appearances for Blackpool in the first and reserve teams but he was only on the winning side on two occasions. He was in the Coca-Cola Cup side that defeated Chelsea 3-1 on 25 September 1996 but then he had to wait until 14 January 1997 before tasting victory again when he was a 79th-minute substitute as Blackpool beat Lincoln City in an Auto Windscreens Shield second round tie. Blackpool released him after just the one season, probably feeling that he was a bad luck charm!

A GENEROUS GESTURE

Blackpool sent their Central League championship side plus Eric Hayward and Willie McIntosh to play Third Division (North) Chester in a benefit game for the home side's long-serving full-back Reg Butcher on 3 May 1950. The Blackpool team was Willie Hall, Gordon Kennedy, Tom Garrett, Walter Jones, Eric Hayward, Ewan Fenton, Albert Hobson, Joe Davies (a Chester player), Willie McIntosh (Cam Burgess, a Chester player, for the second half), Doug Davidson and Rex Adams and they were "faster and more direct than their opponents" and were "pressing for most of the game". It was no surprise, therefore, that they won 4-1 with two goals from Adams and one each from McIntosh and Hobson.

THE BIG FREEZE

The wintry weather claimed a record 42 games on the weekend of 30 December 1961 including the Blackpool versus Sheffield United game scheduled for Bloomfield Road. Stockport referee Mr J S Pickles motored through driving snow on the Friday night to call off Blackpool's game as the pitch was frostbound and snow-covered so there was no hope of a change in conditions. Blackpool officials had him come to the ground early as they had been concerned about the state of the pitch since the Thursday when it was as hard as concrete and, although there was a slight thaw on the Friday, the snow that followed made the surface treacherous. Mr Pickles had intended to make a final decision on the Saturday morning but on arriving at the ground and trying out the conditions he immediately called the game off. Blackpool manager Ron Suart was in complete agreement saying, "Mr Pickles soon realised that it was treacherous under foot and that a player losing his balance and falling on the rock hard ground could seriously hurt himself." The game was eventually played on 3 April 1962 when goals from Ray Parry and Peter Hauser could not save Blackpool from a 4-2 defeat.

CARNIVAL TIME

For their first round FA Cup tie against Sheffield United on 12 January 1924 Blackpool incorporated the stands used on the promenade during the 1923 Carnival Week to augment the accommodation on the popular (east) side of the ground. This added an extra 2,000 reserved seats to the capacity and they sold for five shillings and ninepence (just under 30p) and were available, perhaps surprisingly, from Mr C H Wells' restaurant at 61 Central Drive. Disappointingly the crowd was only 12,567, spectators perhaps put off by the letter that 'Fair Play' wrote to the *Gazette* prior to the game. He wrote, "I must point out the wretched condition of the road leading off Central Drive to the ground, seeing that thousands will be using the road. Surely the club or highway authorities will do something to make the road passable for foot passengers. Do not let the town get a bad name with other parts of the country for ill-paved and dirty streets." Those Seasiders supporters who did attend went home well pleased as a goal from Bert White put them through to round two.

DISASTROUS WEEKEND

The weekend of 8/9 January 1921 proved to be a disastrous one for Blackpool's regular full-backs who had partnered each other for 19 games in the 1920/21 season. Right-back Horace Fairhurst had received a nasty knock on the head in the 1-0 victory over Barnsley on 27 December 1921 while Bert Tulloch travelled to Darlington for the first round FA Cup tie leaving his wife ill in bed at home. Fairhurst was not playing in the game for, having already missed one league game, he was deemed "not recovered sufficiently to run the risk of playing him". Sadly he died from the injury on 9 January 1921. Tulloch arrived back at Blackpool's North Station from the 2-2 draw with Darlington to be greeted with the sad news that his wife had died at eight o'clock that night. On 4 May 1921 a benefit game between Blackpool (Past and Present) and Preston North End was played at Bloomfield Road with the proceeds to go to the widow of Horace Fairhurst and the children of Bert Tulloch. The game was drawn 3-3 and the receipts were £325, which together with a collection made on the ground, resulted in £400 being presented to the beneficiaries.

BLACKPOOL ILLUMINATED

Heart of Midlothian, the Scottish Cup holders, were the visitors to Bloomfield Road when Blackpool officially switched on their floodlights on 13 October 1958. Two goals from Scotsman Jackie Mudie gave Blackpool a 2-1 victory.

SHIRT CHANGE

When Blackpool played Liverpool in a Lancashire Cup tie at Anfield on 22 October 1923, the referee decided that the visitors should change their tangerine shirts so as to avoid a colour clash. Blackpool complained because the decision was made only as the teams lined up to kick off when the referee decided he would be "handicapped and hindered" through the clash of tangerine and red. Blackpool did not take the decision lightly and complained bitterly that they ought not to be made to change as they felt that tangerine and red did not clash as the colours were quite distinctive. They also complained that the colour change to white shirts and black shorts made them "not feel at home", which proved correct as they lost 4-0!

STATISTICS GALORE

In the game against Everton on 24 March 1951 Blackpool did not concede a single corner and the forwards were never offside. Blackpool goalkeeper George Farm took 13 goal kicks while Ted Sagar, his opposite number, took 22. Stan Mortensen scored twice to give Blackpool a 2-0 victory.

MONEY WELL SPENT

At the annual general meeting at the Stanley Arms on 17 May 1920 Blackpool announced that they had spent £3,700 on ground improvements during the 1919/20 season. The statement read, "The committee had carried out many ground improvements last season, especially with regard to stand accommodation, but the gates were such that the directors feel justified in still further increasing the stand accommodation and now the stand on the west side is to be extended to the railway and the ground will be lengthened by the hoarding at the south end being moved nearer to Bloomfield Road." The changes were expected to add a few thousand more to the ground capacity.

DRAWING POWER

The largest crowd to watch Blackpool in a league game was at Stamford Bridge on 16 October 1948 when 77,696 were present to see a 3-3 draw. Locked out were also 30,000 spectators, who had to be disciplined by the mounted police as every road to the ground was blocked. Blackpool, with two goals from Andy McCall and one from Stan Mortensen, were leading 3-1 with five minutes to go but they had Ronnie Suart limping on the wing and Walter Rickett trying desperately to adapt to play full-back. Rickett, probably thinking he was still on the left wing, wandered upfield and Jim Bowie struck twice to earn Chelsea a draw.

ONE STRIKE AND OUT

There was only one Blackpool player on the list of cautions issued by the Football League covering the period 28 August 1937 to 4 December 1937. Jimmy McIntosh was the offender and he had been cautioned in a game against Manchester City reserves on 9 October when it was alleged that he had attempted to strike an opponent.

YOUNGEST

When he made his league debut against Wigan Athletic on 19 August 1989 Trevor Sinclair became Blackpool's youngest ever league player at the age of 16 years and 170 days. The game ended 0-0 and Blackpool manager Jimmy Mullen commented, "Steve McIlhargey, Dave Burgess and young Trevor Sinclair were the only ones I could say came through deserving no criticism. As far as Sinclair is concerned, any 16-year-old making his league debut has to have a good game. He was a boy put in to do a man's job and that isn't really fair on him at such a young age."

NO SPIRITS

Mrs Parr's coffee stall at Bloomfield Road was said to be "a great innovation" when it was opened prior to the Second Division game against Newton Heath on 28 September 1901. 'Geordie' Anderson scored twice for Blackpool but it was not enough to prevent a 4-2 defeat and Blackpool's poor performance had one spectator exclaiming, "It required something stronger in which to drown our sorrows … the members' bar was more in demand!"

NORTH AMERICAN VISITORS

On 4 January 1892 Blackpool entertained the Canadian national side at Raikes Hall, but "the Canadians failed to catch on in Blackpool and Monday's match must have resulted in a loss to the Blackpool club. It has been much the same throughout the tour of the Canadians and there is more than one club lamenting that they took them on. Still the team contains, and did contain, some good players who are worth their salt." Those players did not perform to their potential as Canada were beaten 3-1 by goals from 'Gyp' Cookson, Harry Tyrer and Jimmy Atkinson.

NO JOY RIDE

The *Topical Times* of 7 June 1930 reported "Blackpool are finding it hard to raise their £20,000 Fund. Fancy a club that has won promotion to the First Division having to consider sending out so many appeals for subscriptions. Obviously, the Blackpool officials are soon finding out that entering into the senior division is not going to be a joy ride."

NO ADMITTANCE

Having won the Lancashire League title in the 1893/94 season and finishing runners-up to Fairfield in the following season, Blackpool made an application to join the Second Division of the Football League for the 1895/96 season. Fairfield, Nelson and Accrington were also applying and Lincoln City, Walsall Town Swifts, Burslem Port Vale and Crewe Alexandra were all applying for re-election. The Blackpool directors were doing their utmost to get into the Second Division, had campaigned for election amongst the other clubs and had announced that they would forfeit their £20 Lancashire League fee, which they had already paid, should they be elected. Rivals and fellow Lancashire League club South Shore were not happy with this statement and suggested it would "cause bad blood between them". However, South Shore had no need to be concerned because, with 16 votes, Blackpool were not elected even though Messrs J T Todd, G Gettins, R Swarbrick, J Cox and Whittaker Bond had represented the club at the meeting and had previously canvassed for votes. Lincoln City and Burslem Port Vale, each with 22 votes, were re-elected as were Crewe Alexandra, with 18 votes, and they were joined by Loughborough Town, also with 18 votes.

NINETY-NINE NOT OUT

In the tenth minute of the game against Nottingham Forest on 16 March 1974 Alan Suddick hammered a shot into the net from 30 yards to score what was his 100th league and cup goal. It was a tremendous achievement and the players and manager Harry Potts were eager to share Suddick's moment of joy. However, referee Mr H Williams of Sheffield, having initially awarded the goal, spotted the linesman's flag was raised, went across to consult with him and then disallowed the effort. Potts was well ahead of his time when he commented on the incident as he said, "In my opinion the linesman was correct in signalling, but it is the referee's, not the linesman's, decision to say whether a player is interfering with play. No Blackpool player was committing such an offence when Alan Suddick scored. That is where I fault Mr Williams and say that he should have allowed Alan's goal to count." Suddick had to wait until the following week to complete his century when he scored from a penalty in a 3-0 victory over Preston North End.

'POOL ON PARADE

Blackpool travelled to Barrow's new Parade Ground on 9 September 1893 for a Lancashire League game on the steamship Bickerstaffe, which left from Central Pier. The reason for the mode of transport was that overall it was £4 cheaper than by rail. And of the match a correspondent reported, "Blackpool opened another ground under Lancashire League auspices" but the Barrow club were "not yet educated to Lancashire League standard". Despite a cycling track running across the four corners of the ground and "the grass surface to cinders proving mightily disconcerting to the Blackpool men", they won 5-0 with two goals from Harry Tyrer and one each from Billy Porter, Joe Marsden and Harry Davy. Unfortunately Barrow's sojourn in the Lancashire League was short-lived for, after seven defeats in seven games, they dropped out of the league in November 1893 with their place being taken by Bacup.

NOTHING'S COOKING!

Blackpool were keen to sign Aberdeen forward Charlie Cooke and watched him on a number of occasions before making an offer for him, "a substantial sum, well into five figures", in December 1964. The offer was turned down and Blackpool manager Ronnie Suart commented, "I quoted the figure we were prepared to pay and Mr Pearson's immediate reaction was that they would want at least double what we offered, if not more, for Cooke. We could not see our way to paying what Aberdeen wanted but that is not necessarily the end of the matter. We are still interested in the player and it is now a question of awaiting developments." Cooke signed for Dundee for a fee of £40,000 within a few hours of the Blackpool negotiations breaking down. He eventually moved on to Chelsea where he played over 200 games and won 16 Scottish international caps.

A CLUB OUTING

The Blackpool directors took players and officials on a pre-season outing to the Lake District on 2 August 1928. The party left Bloomfield Road at 9.30am in two coaches and proceeded to Newby Bridge for lunch. From there they went on to Lakeside and sailed to Ambleside. They returned via Kendal where they had tea and arrived back at Bloomfield Road at 9.30pm.

SPANISH SOJOURN

When Birmingham City withdrew from the Costa Del Sol Competition to be held in Malaga on 14 and 15 August 1963, Blackpool were invited to take their place and duly accepted. The Malaga weekly sports paper *Rosaleda* welcomed the club and then gave some rather interesting and erroneous facts about the Seasiders. Their correspondent stated, "Blackpool finished third in the league last season" when actually they finished 13th and added, "Their ground has an official capacity of 48,000." After briefly mentioning some of the club's players and their attributes he finished with "There is no doubt that Blackpool will not be easy opponents and that if Real Madrid wish to get to the final, let nobody doubt it, they will first of all have a tricky task, which may just leave them in the lurch." Blackpool met Real Madrid on 14 August and lost 4-1 so Blackpool had a play-off for third place with French league champions and cup holders Monaco 24 hours later. Goalkeeper Tony Waiters was the Blackpool hero as goals from Pat Quinn and Bruce Crawford earned Blackpool third place with a 2-1 victory. The two-goal lead came in six minutes with the Monaco defence "laboured and hesitant" and thereafter the French forwards took control but Waiters played magnificently to keep them at bay. He saved a penalty but was eventually beaten by a close-range effort from Fouques after 60 minutes.

GOAL DROUGHT

In the 1905/06 season Blackpool failed to score more than two goals in any game until the final match of the season when Clapton Orient were defeated 3-0. They finished with 37 goals in 38 games with Harry Hancock, Jimmy Connor and Ernie Francis leading the way with six each.

PROMISING YOUNGSTERS

A team of Blackpool apprentices "showed good form" and defeated a German side 6-0 in a friendly game on 14 August 1969. The side included youngsters Alan Ainscow, John Curtis, Albert Garland, Stuart Parker and Sean Suddards.

GOALSCORER EXTRAORDINAIRE

In 1926/27 Bill Tremelling had the unusual distinction of leading Blackpool's goalscorers list in both the Football League side and the Central League side. In the Football League he scored 30 goals, and 15 in the Central, and all that from a player who was originally signed as a full-back but who at the season's end was described as "not only a marksman but a true leader of the line".

A MILITARY PRESENCE

Hundreds of soldiers were allowed into Blackpool's Central League game against Stalybridge Celtic on 14 November 1914 at half-price. The move was to encourage those stationed in the town to watch the club in its home games. Sadly it backfired as the game was "as dull as ditchwater" and the press comment was "The Tommies must have gone away with a very poor impression of Blackpool football." The game was drawn 1-1 with the amateur C W S Gregson scoring Blackpool's goal.

AN UNEVEN CONTEST

Blackpool finished the game against Huddersfield Town on 24 January 1914 with only eight men as Ben Green, Tommy Charlton and Billy Rooks had to retire injured. There was at the time "some little difference of opinion as to how far the Huddersfield defenders were responsible for the series of misfortunes that Blackpool suffered". Blackpool finished the game with no formation as the players "just went where the ball was" in their efforts to equalise; they did not do so and Huddersfield won 1-0.

SUPER SUBSTITUTE

On as a late substitute for Alan Ainscow in the Anglo-Italian Cup competition final against Bologna on 12 June 1971, 20-year-old Dennis Wann was inside his own half when he "hit an inch-perfect 30-yard pass to Micky Burns who, taking it in his stride, shrugged off the attentions of two defenders and smashed the ball into the net". It proved to be the goal that won the game 2-1 for Blackpool and had Football League secretary Alan Hardaker saying of the team, "You are one of the finest ambassadors English football has ever had in Europe, both on and off the field."

MUSIC TO PLAY BY!

In September 1923 Major Frank Buckley the Blackpool manager was the prime mover behind the novel idea that a brass band should be formed among Blackpool Football Club supporters and that it would play at matches and "so enliven the proceedings and encourage the Seasiders to victory". Major Buckley was prepared to push the idea for all he was worth and he believed it would be a great success in maintaining and increasing an interest in the club. As such he invited any interested parties to contact him at the club. The intention was for collections to be made at the games to go towards the cost of uniforms and instruments and the intention was that the band, if one was formed, would take bookings from anywhere in the town. Noting this idea, the correspondent of the *Gazette* wondered if the idea would lead to the formation of a Blackpool Football Supporters' Club, something that had been tried once before but which was reported as "coming to an untimely end". The *Gazette* did note that such supporters' clubs were flourishing elsewhere. In the event there were no takers and Major Buckley arranged for the Excelsior Prize Band to attend home games at Bloomfield Road on a voluntary basis but with a collection to help defray expenses. The band, under the direction of Mr W E Taylor, first appeared for the game against Coventry City on 27 October 1923 when the musical selection included marches such as The Golliwog and Pat in America and foxtrots In Sunny Lands, Whistle and Caravan. The music obviously didn't inspire the Blackpool players for the game was lost 3-1 with Matt Barrass scoring the Blackpool goal.

TIME GENTLEMEN PLEASE

Blackpool played South Shore in a friendly game at the Athletics Grounds on 2 January 1899 but only 25 minutes each way was played with a former player of both clubs, 'Gyp' Cookson, as referee. Perhaps it was not surprising that the game was drawn 0-0.

BACK TO THE STRIPES

Blackpool's new light and dark blue striped kit was used for the first time by the Central League side in the game against Preston North End reserves on 26 August 1933. Blackpool lost 2-1.

GOOD CROWDS

In the Second Division promotion season of 1936/37 the average home gate was 17,453. At Central League games it was an encouraging 4,513.

FOR WHOM THE BELL TOLLS

When Bury's 19-year-old wing-half or inside-forward Colin Bell was transfer listed at his own request in February 1966 and was on offer for a fee of £60,000, Blackpool were one of a long list of clubs interested in signing him. The price did not deter manager Ronnie Suart but he did say after ringing Bury manager Bert Head for discussions, "It was only a tentative enquiry - a routine check." Bell had already turned down Bolton Wanderers because he wanted a First Division club but after a week's speculation and strong rumours that Blackpool had put in an offer of £35,000, Head announced, "We have received no offer whatsoever from Blackpool." Bell moved to Manchester City in March 1966 and went on to win 48 England caps.

CONFLICT OF INTERESTS

Blackpool were at home to Lincoln City and South Shore were at home to Clitheroe on 19 February 1898 and the attendances at both games suffered as a consequence. The situation prompted the local press to report, "Football does not enjoy such vogue in Blackpool that when both the local clubs are engaged in town at the same time both gates are not bound to suffer. This was the case on Saturday, and there would not be more than a thousand spectators at the Athletic Grounds to welcome Lincoln City." How many were at South Shore's Cow Gap Lane ground is not reported but gate receipts amounted to £4, "just about enough to pay advertising and other incidental expenses, exclusive of the players' wages". Those spectators that were present were treated to a goal-fest as Blackpool defeated Lincoln City 5-0 in a Second Division game while South Shore defeated Clitheroe 5-1 in the Lancashire League fixture.

PLAYER SHORTAGE

Blackpool had a shortage of players on 14 September 1974: the 'A' team played the game with ten men against Southport reserves and drew 0-0.

BONUS DEAL

For the 1962/63 season Blackpool introduced a bonus system based on attendances at home matches. From the start of the season until the end of the illuminations, at Christmas and at Easter and for any FA Cup ties first-team players were to receive a bonus for every 1,000 spectators over and above a minimum of 23,000 at Bloomfield Road. In addition, during the out of holiday season games, a bonus was to be paid for every 1,000 spectators over and above 15,000. The amount of the bonus was unspecified and a club spokesman commented, "This is the subject of a private contract between the club and the players and it is not for us to divulge it." The players narrowly missed out for the first two home games against Ipswich Town and Wolverhampton Wanderers when the attendances were 23,305 and 23,823 respectively. However the Tottenham Hotspur game on 8 September brought them their first bonus with a crowd of 31,773. Three more games in the holiday periods also brought them a bonus, Manchester City on 22 September, 29,461, Manchester United on 6 October, a best of the season 33,242, and Everton on 13 April, 27,842. And in a season when the average home attendance was 18,536 the players also earned the bonus for a crowd of over 16,000 on six occasions.

LATE ARRIVALS

There were only 4,000 spectators present at Bloomfield Road for the start of the game against Barnsley on Christmas Day 1920, the reason stated being "most people could not get away from their Christmas dinners"! However, once the seasonal repast was over, the crowd swelled to one of 12,000 and "many of the more adventurous climbed on top of the roof of the new grandstand", action that prompted the local press to report, "The directors ought to stop this practice as it could lead to a serious accident some day." In support of this statement it was pointed out "The corrugated iron roofing will not stand an unlimited weight of spectators" and on the day "some parts of the roof sagged in ominous fashion, putting the wind up quite a number of stand occupants". However, all survived with no mishaps and Blackpool made it a Happy Christmas by winning 1-0 with a Jimmy Heathcote goal.

AN UNEXPECTED TIE

On 12 August 1929 Blackpool's players were taken to Ingleton as a pre-season get-together for the purpose of team bonding. After a number of speeches had been made and after lunch had been taken, the players enjoyed a game of cricket, which would have "surprised the MCC for there was no strict adherence to the laws"! For instance 'Jock' Hamilton, who was the jester of the match, was caught off the first ball of the innings when Billy Benton's side went in to bat against a total of 91 made by Bill Tremelling's side. Scotsman Hamilton protested, saying he "hadna' seen the ba' comin'" and was allowed another innings in which he proceeded to hit an adventurous 18. And after Stan Ramsay had "sent the villagers hunting all over the parish for lost balls in a free-hitting innings of 22", victory looked assured. But then disaster came swiftly and remorselessly as Sidney Brooks, who revealed himself as a more than useful medium to fast left-arm bowler, took five wickets in five balls and the services of one or two of the directors had to be sought. In the end, Mr S Butterworth, the club chairman, was bowled three times in one over by Brooks but mysteriously while he was at the crease the total had crept up to 91 and the game was tied!

THE BEST LAID PLANS ...

Non-league Colchester United were the giantkillers of the 1948 FA Cup when they knocked out league clubs Huddersfield Town and Bradford Park Avenue en route to a fifth-round tie with Blackpool at Bloomfield Road on 7 February 1948. Ted Fenton, Colchester's player-manager, visited Blackpool a week before the tie and made notes while watching a 1-1 draw with Aston Villa. He later boasted that he had designed an 'M' plan to stop Matthews and Mortensen. He said the plan was "to put them in chains", adding, "Everyone knows that Matthews and Mortensen are great footballers – I played with them and against them in Forces games during the war – but a wonderful fellow named Doherty played for Huddersfield." And he stressed, "Doherty was successfully eliminated." However, his plans for Blackpool did not bear fruit as his gallant side, with only four professional players, lost 5-0 and all the goals came from the 'M' players, Mortensen and McIntosh, two each, and Munro.

BAD BEHAVIOUR

Having scored his side's goal in what turned out to be a 2-1 defeat, Blackpool's Bob Whittingham was sent off in a reserve game against Manchester City on 18 January 1908 at Bloomfield Road for what was described by one correspondent as "a trivial foul on Buckley". The referee, Mr T E Hargreaves of Liverpool, had not previously spoken to Whittingham but he deemed what was reported as "merely a backheel" a sending-off offence. The crowd were incensed and when the referee left the field he was pelted with mud and cinders and was "freely hooted". After the game the referee, "accompanied by a policeman or two", left the ground by the northerly exit, unmolested, and was escorted across the fields to Revoe! A meeting of the Lancashire Football Association on 24 January reviewed the situation and a spectator who had manhandled the referee was in attendance with the Blackpool officials. The spectator apologised to the LFA committee and Blackpool were ordered to provide a private entrance to the dressing rooms for the visiting teams and officials, or to see that the passages leading to the rooms were kept clear of spectators until the players and officials were safely in their respective dressing rooms. The club also had to pay the expenses of the witnesses that had been called and in addition Whittingham received an official caution.

EASTER JOY

When Blackpool played at Darwen in a Second Division game on Good Friday 31 March 1899, the home side began the game with only nine men. The score was still 0-0 when the other two players eventually arrived but Blackpool went on to win 6-0 with two goals from Jack Morris and one each from Harry Parr, Jack Parkinson, Bob Birket and Frank Williams.

A ROUND DOZEN

There was a goal-fest at Bloomfield Road on 27 September 1952 when Blackpool entertained Charlton Athletic when a crowd of 33,498 gathered to see the Seasiders' highest Football League score. It was 5-1 at half-time and midway through the second half it was 8-1 before Blackpool relaxed and allowed Charlton to score three more to make the final score 8-4. The goals came from Allan Brown, three, Stan Mortensen, Ernie Taylor, Tommy Garrett, Stan Matthews and a Hammond own goal.

STAN MATTHEWS SCORES BLACKPOOL'S SEVENTH GOAL IN THEIR HIGHEST LEAGUE SCORE, CHARLTON ATHLETIC BEATEN 8-4 ON 27 SEPTEMBER 1952.

SNEAK THIEVES

After Blackpool had lost 2-1 to Bradford City at Bloomfield Road on 10 April 1925 in front of the largest home crowd of the season, 17,000, George Mee, Jack Meredith and Harry Bedford discovered that they had been robbed when changing in the dressing room under the West Stand after the game. Meredith lost £15 and Mee and Bedford lost gold pocket watches, with Bedford having one of his international medals attached to his watch. The Blackpool directors immediately called in the police but there was no sign of the thieves, who had obviously taken advantage of the game being in progress to commit the robbery. Amazingly, Mee's watch was found the following morning by a pedestrian who discovered it wrapped in newspaper in a pillar box.

TWELFTH MAN

An attendance of nearly 6,000 saw Blackpool lose a Lancashire League game at Chorley 2-1 on 1 January 1900 even though the home side played the whole of the second half with only ten men. Late in the first half the game "became very rough" and two Chorley players had to leave the field; one returned but one was unable to do so. However, one correspondent reported, "but the referee supplied the deficiency" and then added, "[he] quickly began to make himself obnoxious". Walton, a former South Shore player, had scored Chorley's two goals and Bob Birket had replied for Blackpool before the Seasiders had one last chance to equalise but as Birket was about to put the ball into the net, he was "kicked completely off his feet". It seemed a clear-cut penalty to all but the referee who thought otherwise and, to everyone's dismay, awarded a free kick to Chorley! Birket was carried off and Blackpool slipped to defeat.

RESERVE RECORD

A record crowd of 23,605 watched the Central League game between Preston North End reserves and Blackpool reserves at Deepdale on 6 May 1938. The reason for the huge crowd was that the triumphant Preston first team who had won the FA Cup a week earlier by defeating Huddersfield Town 1-0 at Wembley were parading the cup round the ground. As for the supporting cast, Preston won the reserve game 1-0.

CAPTURED IN VERSE

When Blackpool lost 3-1 to Southampton in the second round of the FA Cup on 2 February 1924 one supporter was so upset that he put his thoughts into verse. Fred Buckley of 25 Kensington Road wrote:

Good-bye/Cup tie,/Blackpool's out!/Some day/We may/Elsewhere shout.
Don't fret/Or let/Hope expire;/Set to,/Win through/To League higher.
This plan/Will come/('Tis no match)/With score/One more/Every match.
Good-bye/Cup tie,/Good-bye, Cup!/Take heart,/Be smart,/Then move up!

A little bit of doggerel that very much said that, having been dismissed from the FA Cup, the club could then concentrate on the league! And Blackpool made a brave attempt at promotion to the First Division by finishing fourth on 49 points behind champions Leeds United, 54 points, and Bury and Derby County, both 51 points.

A REAL LIVE DOLL

Blackpool introduced a Miss Tangerine doll as a souvenir for supporters at the start of the 1973/74 season but there was also a matching real live living doll. Supporter Wendy Langstone adopted the crinoline style gown of the souvenir doll and acted as the football club's ambassador in various venues around the town. She wore a tangerine crinoline gown that had been made by Mrs Marjorie Martin out of 25 yards of taffeta with an underskirt to match and with 13 and a half yards of trimming, all hand sewn, to decorate it and the outfit was topped off with a poke bonnet. The gown took Mrs Martin 80 hours to complete but Wendy was a wow when she appeared around town on promotional visits and especially when she paraded round the ground prior to every home game.

GIMMICKS GALORE

Blackpool kicked off the 1996/97 season in style against Chesterfield on 17 August 1996. A helicopter brought in the match ball and there were performers on stilts and jugglers to entertain the early arrivals. In addition there was music and a giant video wall to mark what was called 'Cable Day', celebrating Blackpool's six-figure sponsorship deal with Telewest Communications. However, Chesterfield spoiled the party by winning 1-0.

PUBLIC UNEASE

The last Saturday of the aborted 1939/40 season, 2 September 1939, saw attendances at matches drop considerably as the public were uneasy about the possibility of war. Indeed, there were only three grounds that attracted an attendance of 20,000 or more, Blackpool, 22,000, and Birmingham and Cardiff, 20,000 each.

A VETERAN PLAYER

Probably the oldest player to make his league debut for Blackpool was outside-left George 'Jud' Harrison who played his first game for the Seasiders in a 2-1 defeat by Sheffield Wednesday on 14 November 1931 at the age of 39 years 120 days. Harrison had already had a long and distinguished career with Leicester Fosse, Everton and Preston North End for whom he had played a combined total of 510 league games, scoring 99 goals. He had also won two England international caps before Blackpool signed him on a free transfer from Preston on 10 November 1931. He remained at Bloomfield Road for just one season, playing in 15 league games and scoring two goals before retiring to become a publican, firstly at the Moorbank Inn in Preston and then at the Rising Sun Hotel in his home town of Church Gresley.

EVENING KICK-OFF

Blackpool kicked off their reserve game against Leeds United reserves on 4 September 1922 in the early evening (before the advent of floodlights) but a crowd of only 3,000 watched Jack Leaver score twice to give the home side a 2-1 victory. Such a disappointing attendance was deemed "not to encourage the directors to play the games in the evenings". And they did not do so thereafter.

FORTUITOUS FOG

Fog descended and caused the abandonment of Blackpool's reserve game at Bury after 47 minutes on 2 January 1909 when Bury were winning 4-0. The game was replayed at Gigg Lane on 9 April 1909 and Blackpool won 2-1!

STAR CRICKETERS

On 15 August 1929 a team of Blackpool footballers entertained Essex Wanderers, a touring side, at cricket at Whitegate Park. The Essex side were undefeated with four wins and a draw in their five matches on tour but they met their match with the footballers winning comfortably. The visitors were dismissed for just 98 with Percy Downes leading the bowlers with 4-17, Bill Tremelling taking 3-10 and guest player Vic Norbury, formerly of Hampshire and Lancashire, taking 2-21. In reply Blackpool passed the Essex total in just 45 minutes and with the loss of only two wickets and they went on to finish with 154-9. Opening batsman Jack Oxberry top scored with 75, made in only 55 minutes while Syd Tufnell made 25 not out and Jimmy Hampson 18.

A MISSED OPPORTUNITY

Henry 'Gyp' Cookson was unlucky not to become Blackpool Football Club's first England international in 1891 when a telegram was sent to Blackpool asking, "Can Cookson play for England?" The game in question was to be one arranged by the English Association's Mr J J Bentley against the touring Canadian team. Unfortunately the telegram was wrongly delivered, to Mr Albert Hargreaves, later connected with Blackpool Football Club but then the secretary of another local team, Blackpool Olympic. The delay in getting the message to the Blackpool secretary Mr George Whittaker meant that Cookson missed his chance of an international cap as Blackpool had "an important fixture" against Bury at Gigg Lane for which Cookson was required. Cookson was particularly unlucky because it was the second time that he had missed out on a possible England international cap after Football Association officials had noted his skilful play for South Shore in the 1889/90 season. As a consequence he was chosen as reserve for the England team to play Ireland and he was to play should the fitness of centre forward Jack Southworth of Blackburn Rovers be called into question. The local news, understandably welcomed in the Fylde, was that Southworth would be unable to play due to a knee injury and Gyp's chances of a first international cap looked extremely healthy. However, there was a dispute between the FA and the Irish FA and the game was postponed so Cookson missed out on his opportunity.

PAY DAY

For the first time in the club's history a five per cent dividend for shareholders was announced at the annual general meeting on 17 May 1920 after a profit of £3,720 had been made in the 1919/20 season.

FOURTH TIME LUCKY

Blackpool chased Bob Stokoe to become manager in November 1970 but his club Carlisle United would have none of it. However persistence eventually paid off for the Seasiders when on 29 December 1970, after secret negotiations between the two clubs, Carlisle agreed to release Stokoe to take over at Bloomfield Road but the Carlisle chairman Mr George Sheffield would not state whether the £8,500 transfer fee that his club had originally demanded had been paid, stating only "Amicable arrangements have been agreed with Blackpool." Stokoe was to be paid £7,000 a year and he commented, "I am very happy. This is something I have wanted and fought for. I wanted a chance to better myself." And in January 1971, after he had been in the job for a short time and was, according to reports, "up to his ears in crises" as Blackpool fought to avoid relegation from the First Division, he commented, "Every manager, I don't care who he is, wants to have a crack with a First Division side. When Blackpool came to me for the fourth time I knew I had to go. I could hardly expect any of the very top clubs to come; they just don't part with their managers anyway."

NO GIANT KILLERS

Blackpool's hopes of an FA Cup run were cruelly dashed in December 1907 when the draw for the first round paired them with Manchester United, at the time nicknamed 'the team of talent'. United were top of the First Division with 14 wins and two defeats in their 16 games and with 50 goals scored and only 21 conceded; Second Division Blackpool meanwhile had only won two and drawn five of their 15 games with 23 goals scored and 30 conceded. One Manchester writer assessed the tie with "It would be a case of David slaying Goliath were Blackpool to beat Manchester United at Bank Street, where the present League leaders have not so much as forfeited a point." And there was no giant killing act by Blackpool who lost 3-1 on 11 January 1908 with 'Alty' Grundy scoring the consolation goal.

'WIENER BLUT' – VIENNESE BLOOD

Blackpool's first European opposition was FC Wien [Vienna] who were entertained at Bloomfield Road on 9 December 1935 when the two clubs shared the gate receipts after deduction of entertainment tax and all match expenses. The kick-off was 2.15pm and admission prices were the same as for first-team games. FC Wien fielded four Austrian internationals and a 5,000 crowd saw Blackpool come from 1-0 down to win an exciting game 4-3 with the goals scored by Tom Jones, Dickie Watmough, Jimmy McIntosh, his first senior goal for the club, and Peter Doherty. The net financial gain for each club was £127 17s 4d. The FC Wien party, which had visited places of interest in the town prior to the game, were entertained to a dinner after the match at the County Hotel where Blackpool's vice-chairman Mr Butterworth congratulated the Austrians on the good football that they had played and commented, "These Austrian footballers have come on an embassy of friendliness from their own country to ours, recognising that sport is the greatest peacemaker in the world. I am happy to give an official, but nevertheless sincere, 'Welcome and well played' to our visitors from Vienna." In reply, the Vienna manager Herr Max Cernic, the only visitor who could speak English [there was a translator for the others], expressed his club's appreciation and said, "We all know the great importance of football in the relationships between the peoples of the world. Football has been called a great peacemaker. There is a word for 'peacemaker' in our language. It is freely translated 'evangelist of sport'. It is as 'evangelists of sport' that we come to you, and we can only say that if our football has satisfied you, no greater distinction could be bestowed on us."

CANINE CAPERS

A dog, owned by Blackpool Football Club, that guarded the ground went wandering unattended on 29 December 1913 and was picked up by a police constable in Lytham when it was, in his words, "at large after sunset"! It had a tag on it that stated that it belonged to Tommy Barcroft of the football club. A summons was issued but after discussion of the case on 22 January 1914, the charge was withdrawn with the explanation "There seems to have been a mishap."

RETRIBUTION

On 4 December 1943 Blackpool played Oldham Athletic and in the first half the tough-tackling former Blackpool full-back Tommy Shipman gave Stan Matthews a torrid time. At half-time he complained to 'Jock' Dodds in the dressing room and asked Dodds if there was anything he could do. In Dodds' own words, "Leave it to me, Stan." And he duly went out and in the first minutes of the second half clattered Shipman onto the cinder track. Realising what he had done Dodds went down as though he too was injured, but, again in his own words, "I was shamming because I knew the referee would not be happy. Anyway he walked over to me as I was writhing on the ground and asked if I was okay. 'Yes, I think so,' I replied. 'Well, can you walk?' he asked. I said that I thought so and he simply said, 'Well, walk off down the tunnel because I'm sending you off!'" Dodds was duly dismissed and on 1 January 1944 he was "very strongly warned" by the FA Disciplinary Committee following his reported undue robust play against Oldham.

THE 'GENE KELLY' STAND

In the early days of Blackpool Football Club the east side of the ground was known as the 'popular side' and beginning in the 1924/25 season Blackpool Supporters' Club began to raise money to provide a stand on that side of the ground. A Ladies' Committee, under the chairmanship of Miss L Furber and with Miss Gallagher as secretary, was formed to raise additional money for the project and in March 1926 a contract was signed for the erection of the stand, which was estimated to cost £2,300. The word 'stand' was taken to mean at that time, terracing specifically with a roof over it and early in the 1926/27 season it was reported, "An outstanding event during the season [1925/26] was the ambitious proposal of the supporters' club to erect a cover over the 'popular' (east) side of the ground. The first part of the scheme has now been completed at a cost of £2,200." A supporters' club spokesman said, "The man who pays his 'bob' [one shilling or 5p] will be able to watch the game in comfort" and on behalf of the club's directors, Albert Hindley thanked the supporters' club for "a magnificent gift".

HARSH JUSTICE

Blackpool and Aston Villa were both fined ten guineas [£10.50] by The Football League in August 1938 for approaching Thomas Whalley while that player was a registered league player with Oldham Athletic. Blackpool felt aggrieved as they had signed Whalley on West Lancashire League forms on 7 February 1938 and he had played one or two games for the club at that level before being signed by Oldham Athletic on a Football League amateur form.

THE SWEET SMELL OF SUCCESS

Blackpool were short of funds during the 1922/23 season and the ladies associated with the club had made many efforts to raise money with whist drives and other social events but for the game against Bury on 14 April 1923 a Miss Waddicor of Princess Street came up with a novel idea. She organised a flower day for the club and spectators were asked to purchase and wear a small spray of Lilies of the Valley in the club's colours. The day was a success and Blackpool made it doubly so by defeating Bury 5-1 with the goals coming from Harry Bedford, three, Jack Charles and Matt Barrass.

THE GREEN

Blackpool's popular football newspaper that eventually became *The Green* first appeared as an *Evening Gazette Football Final* on 31 August 1929 when the newsvendors' cry around the town was "Football Final! Read All About It!" The advance advertising for the newspaper claimed, "Within a short time of the final whistle, the Football Edition of the *Evening Gazette* will be selling in newsagents' shops and on the streets of Blackpool and the Fylde. It will contain accounts of all the leading matches with special attention to the League games of the Blackpool club. Reports will be telephoned direct from Bloomfield Road over our private telephone by our football expert. He will accompany the Blackpool football team on its away fixtures and his accounts will be telephoned direct into the head office at Blackpool. Reports and all the results of the matches in the various Leagues, and the corrected League tables will be published without delay. THE PRICE WILL BE ONE PENNY." *The Green* was to flourish for over 50 years.

ON LOAN

In the 2008/09 season Blackpool signed 19 loan players. They were Sone Aluko, Mo Camara, Alan Gow, Graham Stack, Zesh Rehman, Steve Kabba, Kristian Nemmeth, Charlie Adam, DJ Campbell, Graeme Owens, Roy O'Donovan, Nick Blackman, Adam Hammill, Liam Dickinson, Wade Small, Alan Mahon, Lee Hendrie, Paul Marshall and Kyel Reid.

IT'S BETTER BY AIR

Blackpool became the first Football League club to fly to a fixture on the day of the game when they flew in a Dakota bound for Rhoose Airport, near Cardiff on Friday 24 March 1961. The Football League had always been opposed to clubs flying on the day of the game in case of uncertain weather but Alan Hardaker, secretary of the Football League stated, "Before I put Blackpool's application to the management committee, the club gave me an assurance that they would prepare alternative travelling arrangements to ensure getting to Cardiff in time for the kick-off in the event of the flight being cancelled." The club took every precaution to prevent any problems by checking the weather forecast the night before the flight and on the morning of it. Had conditions not been favourable, a coach had been arranged to take the team to Preston in time to catch a train for Cardiff. Richard Seed, secretary of the club, said, "Like all other clubs, we will be faced with heavy increases in expenditure next season with the abolition of the maximum wage and we feel that by flying to long distance matches wherever possible, we shall be able to reduce the big expenditure incurred by overnight stops." Blackpool won the game 2-0 with goals from Ray Charnley and Des Horne to ease their relegation fears.

NO NUMBER ONE

The numbering of players' shirts was introduced into league football for the 1939/40 season and at Blackpool it was announced, "The numbers are in white on the backs of the jerseys. Number 2 is the right-back, number 3 the left-back through to number 11 for the outside-left. There is no number for goalkeepers but next season for the first time there will be the coat of arms shield on the jerseys of Blackpool goalkeepers." The club's trainers would wear "tangerine sweaters and blue blazers".

BLACKPOOL EVEN FLEW THE SIDE TO A CENTRAL LEAGUE GAME AT NEWCASTLE ON 26 MARCH 1960!

REFEREE NOT REQUIRED

Blackpool's game against Newcastle United on 21 December 1935 was in doubt all week due to a heavy frost and 50 tons of sand had been scattered over the iron-clad grass by a gang summoned to the ground at first light on the morning of the game. Then a dense fog suddenly descended as the Newcastle players arrived at the ground. Meanwhile Mr W R Jennings, the referee, had boarded his train in brilliant sunshine in York but when it crossed the Lancashire border it became fog-bound and limped on to Poulton. At Poulton Mr Jennings was admitted to an empty first-class carriage where he changed before taking a taxi to Bloomfield Road where he arrived ten minutes before the scheduled kick-off time. To his surprise he found the gates closed, less than 2,000 people huddled outside the ground and, more pertinently, that his linesmen had already called off the game.

A SMOKY ATMOSPHERE

For the start of the 1925/26 season a new directors' box was on view in the West Stand at Bloomfield Road for the opening game against Southampton on 29 August, which Blackpool won 2-1 with goals from Jack Meredith and Harry Bedford. The directors "took up their places like a lot of jurymen waiting for double fees" and the new box had Ernest Lawson writing in the *Gazette & Herald*, "It's a nice box they have placed themselves in; it must be for safety, for it is far enough out of the way." He then, tongue-in-cheek, posed the question, "But of what are they frightened?" He answered it himself with "The Let Me Be Smoke railway stokers are a choking nuisance. Now we know from what the directors are protecting themselves, but it is time they wrote and asked for the nuisance to be abolished", referring to the smoke that regularly drifted in and across the ground from the north-west corner of the ground. However, the crowd often had "the last laugh on these stokers when the wind is in the east". An unacknowledged poem was penned as a by-product of these comments that went: Then up came Billy Benton,/The captain of the crew;/He gave the ball a gay good munch/And showed them what to do./The stoker on the engine/Filled up his dirty flue/With all the filthy smoke he could/To spoil our two-bob view.

APPEAL UPHELD

Blackpool had a dispute with Chorley over a Lancashire Senior Cup tie due to be played on 9 January 1904 because the Seasiders had a league game with Barnsley on that date and, having no reserve side at the time, could not field a side. Chorley were asked to agree to change the date and Blackpool suggested that it be played at Bloomfield Road on 4 January. When Chorley disagreed, Blackpool offered £20 and half the gate receipts over and above £35 as a further incentive, which would have guaranteed Chorley at least £25. However, Chorley wanted a minimum £30, which Blackpool felt was too extravagant so the game had to be played on the due date. Blackpool fielded a scratch side that was Moran, Robinson, Fletcher, Wolstenholme, Crabtree, Hughes, Miller, Rooke, Hoyle, Jones and Wright and duly lost the game 3-1. Blackpool were not happy and subsequently appealed to the Lancashire Football Association who upheld the appeal that was heard on 13 January. The game was replayed at a neutral ground, Deepdale, when Blackpool, with a full strength team, won 2-0 with goals from Marshall McEwan and Charlie Bennett. Blackpool went out in the next round, losing 2-1 to Manchester United.

NO DUTCH TREAT

Utrecht-born Eric Orie was signed by Blackpool from Austria Vienna on a month's trial in August 1996. When he was named in the side for his first game, a pre-season friendly against Grimsby Town on 3 August, spectators were asking "Eric who?" By the end of the game they were chanting his name as he had scored Blackpool's second goal in a 2-2 draw when "swivelling and sweeping a left foot shot high into the net". He played 77 minutes of the friendly against Falkirk and then made his official debut in the first-round Coca-Cola Cup tie against Scunthorpe United on 20 August when Blackpool disappointingly lost 2-1. After the game manager Gary Megson commented, "I have not sat down with Eric yet but as soon as there is a decision, it will be made public." Megson was true to his word for on 23 August 1996 he announced, "I am not taking it any further with Eric Orie" and the player was on his way back to his Utrecht home after a very brief Bloomfield Road career.

REFURBISHED GROUND

The 1926/27 season opened at Bloomfield Road with "a new grandstand, offices and dressing rooms at the south end of the ground, a new Supporters' Club covered stand on the easterly side, a re-turfed pitch, and other sundry changes such as imposing barricadings, and new turnstiles and alterations which will be to the benefit of the public generally."

NO FLOWERS REQUIRED

Blackpool reached the third round proper of the English [FA] Cup on 24 February 1906 but were beaten 5-0 by high-flying First Division side Newcastle United. Blackpool supporters were quick to produce a funeral card that read: No flowers required./In Loving Memory of Blackpool,/ Who died today,/Gone but not forgotten./Poor Blackpool have departed/ With their supporters all downhearted/For the lads in black and white,/ Have won the great Cup fight,/They are boastful of the day/For Blackpool all the way/Have come and been defeated/By the champions of the day/ Weep not, but be content,/The Cup for you was never meant.

OWNERS AT LAST

Having initially rented the Bloomfield Road ground, Blackpool Football Club purchased it outright in June 1920. As a consequence more money was required to bring the ground up to standard to host First Division football and, therefore, a new share issue was launched. However, for supporters who did not wish to subscribe to the shares the club announced that the early purchase of season tickets would also swell the club's coffers. Prices for the 1920/21 season were £1 for the ground, £2 'B' and Motor Stand, £3 centre stand and £5 for reserved seats (of which there were only a few) in the centre stand. The tickets were available from Ed Little at the Promenade and West Street or from any of the directors.

RECORD SALES

Returning to the First Division for 1937/38, Blackpool generated £6,475 in season ticket sales, a record to that time.

THE KING

There have been many great players down the years at Blackpool but only one of them has ever been elevated to royal status and recognised as the King of Bloomfield Road and that was the mercurial Alan Suddick. He was so revered that the fans made up a song about him, which was sang to the tune of the 16th-century Christmas carol The First Noel. The words of the Alan Suddick version are:

The very first goal that Suddick did score/Made the South Stand cheer and the Spion Kop roar/And from that day we proclaimed him King/Forever he'll reign and forever we'll sing … /Suddick, Suddick, Suddick, Suddick/Born is the King of Bloomfield Road./Immortal, immaculate, Suddick is King/He makes them, he scores them/He rules everything/He sizzles and sparkles/In the sun, wind and wet/He curls them and bends them/Straight into the net … Suddick, Suddick, Suddick, Suddick/Born is the King of Bloomfield Road.

Sadly Alan Suddick died, aged 64, on 16 March 2009 and at the following home game the crowd gave a rendition of the 'King of Bloomfield Road' anthem as a tribute to the great man.

AN EARLY INTERNATIONAL APPEARANCE

Stephen 'Mandy' Hill had made only 27 league appearances spread over three seasons when he was selected for the England Under-23 side against Israel at Elland Road on 9 November 1961. He scored in England's 7-1 victory and went on to play three further Under-23 games.

PROPHETIC REMARK

Shortly after full-back Tommy Garrett had re-signed for Blackpool for the 1946/47 season, and before he had played a league game for the club, Harry Evans, Blackpool's chairman, on his way back from a game in the south, commented, "We've just signed a young full-back who one day will play for England." Prophetic remark it was, for five years later Garrett won the first of his three England caps in the 1951/52 season when he made his debut against Scotland. He then played against Italy later in 1951/52 and against Wales in the 1953/54 season. He also he went on an FA tour to South America.

ABSENTEE MANAGER

Blackpool chairman Sir Lindsay Parkinson suggested in March 1934 that the team manager, at the time 'Sandy' McFarlane, should attend every first-team match. His comment followed a disappointing 1-1 draw with Bolton Wanderers on 24 March, which was Blackpool's fourth game without a win.

LAST MAN STANDING

Following a 2-2 draw with Everton on 6 November 2010, manager Ian Holloway made ten changes for the midweek game with Aston Villa; only Keith Southern from the Everton game was in the starting eleven. Blackpool lost the game 3-2 to a last-minute goal and Holloway was criticised in many quarters. He commented, "I'm a football manager – I don't work for the Premier League." And he added, "If the Premier League want to sit down with me and talk, then fine. I'll happily do that whenever and wherever they want, and I can explain what I did every step of the way. But I'm not having anyone telling me who I should pick and I stick by what I said straight after the game. I am deadly serious about considering resigning if we are fined. I am absolutely not expecting to hear anything from the Premier League. Why would they want to fine us when we are doing so well? I feel offended by all this. I am paid to be manager of Blackpool FC and I used my 25-man squad to its best advantage. If we had lost 10-0 I would maybe accept it was a weak team. But don't call this a weak team – it was a new team I had kept under wraps." Ironically he made 11 changes for the following Saturday's game against West Ham United. The result? A 0-0 draw. The Premier League announced a £25,000 fine in January 2011.

A TALENTED TALENT SCOUT

Blackpool's scout in the north east Ralph Hepplewhite had a very successful run in spotting players over the years. He recommended Jack Charles, Jimmy Jones, Joe Clennell, Levy Thorpe, Bobby Booth, Peter Quinn, Albert Watson, Billy Richardson, Bert Tulloch, Billy Rooks, Monty Wilkinson, Jimmy Kidd, Tommy Buchan, Jack Sibbald and Joe Lane to Bloomfield Road. They were all relatively unknown at the time of the recommendation but all were destined to achieve fame with Blackpool.

THE MAGNIFICENT SEVEN

The first game of the 1973/74 season against West Bromwich Albion on 25 August saw a magnificent seven line-up of Miss Tangerine and her six maids. The Misses Wendy Langstone, Alison Froggatt, Estelle Robinson, Janice Smith, Julie Craig, Debbie Lord and Hazel Webster, suitably attired in tangerine and white, paraded before the kick-off but their presence did 'Pool no good as they went down 3-2.

THEY THINK IT'S ALL OVER

After 90 minutes of the League Cup second round replay against Leeds United at Bloomfield Road on 5 October 1960 the referee, Mr F V Stringer of Liverpool, started to take the players of the field with the score 1-1. Some of the players were almost in the dressing room and some youngsters were on the pitch when Blackpool's assistant manager Eric Hayward rushed on to the field to inform the referee that there had to be a result so extra time had to be played. The extra 30 minutes went against Blackpool as Leeds won 3-1.

HONOURABLE MENTION

Full-back John Bibby, who played between 1892 and 1897, later fought in the Boer War as a sergeant with the 57th Company (Bucks) of the 15th Battalion, machine gun section and he was mentioned in dispatches on 10 September and 27 September 1901. As a consequence he was awarded the Distinguished Conduct Medal but was later discharged from the Army, being medically unfit due to a wound received in action. On his return home he was said to be "a physical wreck, broken in health and body". Sadly he died from the effects of his wounds, aged 34, on 8 April 1902 and was given a military funeral in Blackpool.

OFF THE ROAD

At a board meeting on 22 July 1929 the Blackpool directors decided that no players should drive motor cars or motor cycles during the playing season owing to the risk of injury and a letter stating this was sent to each player!

BACK IN THE BIG TIME

After finishing bottom of Division Two in the 1912/13 season Blackpool had to apply for re-election along with the next to bottom club Stockport County. Chesterfield, Darlington, Gainsborough Trinity, Nelson, South Shields and Stalybridge Celtic all applied for election and the salient question on everyone's lips was "What can the new clubs offer that the ancient allies, Blackpool and Stockport County, cannot supply?" The answer was obviously "Nothing" because Blackpool and Stockport County were re-elected.

FIRST OFFENCE

Never having been booked in his 31 games for Blackpool to that date, full-back Steve Harrison incurred the wrath of the referee against Bristol City on 23 November 1974 when he was sent off. Harrison stated that he was simply trying to wrest himself free from the hold of a Bristol player but the referee saw it differently and dismissed him. Manager Harry Potts commented, "The alleged offence was uncharacteristic of this grand young full-back." Blackpool won the game 1-0 with a Dave Hatton penalty.

A MODEST PROFIT

At their home game with Burslem Port Vale on 24 September 1898 Blackpool took £19 10s 0d (£19.50) in gate receipts while their wage bill for the week was £14.

LATE ON PARADE

On his league debut against Gainsborough Trinity on 21 December 1901 at Bloomfield Road, Blackpool's outside-right Billy Anderton arrived late and "the game had been going on five minutes when he walked on the field". Notwithstanding, Blackpool won 3-0.

CONTRASTING FORTUNES

In August 1947 Blackpool printed 2,000 season tickets and they were all quickly sold. This was quite a contrast to the 1946/47 season when 750 had been printed and hundreds had been left unsold.

THE WORST EVER?

Cowlairs-born forward George McLay was signed by Blackpool on 20 January 1897 when he stated that he had been selected for Scotland in 1894 but that he had been unable to turn out due to injury. However, it quickly became apparent that he was not up to the task and seven days after signing he was told that his services were no longer required. But on 30 January 1897 one of the Blackpool players did not turn up for a Lancashire Combination game against Blackburn Rovers reserves at Raikes Hall. And McLay "pleaded hard for the opportunity to show his worth" so he was given an opportunity. In the game he was "a rank failure" for, as a forward, he "did not appear to have the faintest conception of modern methods of attack". With the crowd baying for his removal, he was pushed back to half-back but unfortunately he was "not one whit better in that position" and was deemed "worse than useless". Blackpool suffered a 5-1 defeat and not surprisingly he was given his "marching orders".

SPECTATOR INTERVENTION

In the home game with Newton Heath on 23 March 1901, Blackpool's goal, scored by Bob Birket, nearly wasn't allowed. It happened when "Birket very smartly headed the ball into the net from a centre by Boulton, and it rolled out at an aperture in the back. The Heathens stoutly maintained that the ball had gone outside the post, and it was placed for a goal kick." It was then that the spectators got involved: "It was left to the youngsters, assembled in strong force around the visitors' goal, to raise their protest, which was unmistakable, and after an inspection of the net and a consultation with both linesmen, the goal was allowed by the referee." It turned out to be academic as Blackpool lost 2-1 after Stirzaker missed a penalty.

MARRIAGE A LA MODE

When Jimmy Hampson married his childhood sweetheart Betty Davies at Walkden Primitive Methodist Church, Little Hulton, on 19 May 1930, the directors of Blackpool Football Club presented the couple with a cake in the shape of half a football field, marked out and with 11 players in tangerine and white as decoration.

HAT-TRICK HEROES

For a period in the 1983/84 season there was a sudden spate of Blackpool hat-tricks. After the club had gone over two seasons without a player scoring three goals in a game there were four hat-tricks in the space of 12 games between 20 March 1984 and 7 May 1984. The sequence began with Nigel Walker, on his debut on a month's loan from Sunderland, scoring three in the 5-1 demolition of Northampton Town on 20 March. Paul Stewart then scored all three goals in the 3-3 draw with Chester City on 24 March and the third hat-trick came from John Deary who scored all Blackpool's goals in the 3-1 victory over Hereford United on 28 April. Finally Ian Britton scored three in the 4-0 win against Halifax Town on 7 May.

EVO-PRESENT

After 26 games of the 2010/11 Premier League season Ian Evatt was the only Blackpool player to feature in all of them. In addition he was the highest ranked Seasider on the EA Sports Player Performance Index in 26th place. He had made 63 clearances and 32 interceptions while also having four goal assists. 'Evo' who was the rock of the Blackpool defence earned himself the nickname 'The Kaiser', after the great Franz Beckenbauer, for his cultured football played from the back.

TWO FOR THE PRICE OF ONE

When Blackpool were chasing 16-year-old Dick Withington from South Shields Ex-Schoolboys, the manager of that team suggested that if the Seasiders were to sign Withington they had also to sign his partner Stan Mortensen. Blackpool were unsure and although they gave Withington a trial, they kept their options open on Mortensen. However, after South Shields Ex-Schoolboys had played a friendly game against a team of Blackpool youngsters at Bloomfield Road over Easter 1938, the club agreed to sign the pair with Withington as their main target and Mortensen a makeweight. The deal cost Blackpool £70, £20 in expenses towards the friendly game and a £50 donation to the club. The rest is history as Withington made no official league appearances for the club, playing only in wartime and in 14 Central League games before being released, while Mortensen went on to greatness.

DICK WITHINGTON (LEFT) AND STAN MORTENSEN PICTURED ON THE DAY THAT THEY SIGNED FOR BLACKPOOL.

A SURFEIT OF GOALKEEPERS

Blackpool used 25 different players in the Division Four campaign of 1983/84. It was, however, somewhat unusual for five of those players to have been goalkeepers. Billy O'Rourke, on loan from Burnley, began the season and played six games. On O'Rourke's return to Burnley Simon Steele was signed on loan from Brighton and Hove Albion and played three games. He then returned to Brighton and Barry Siddall was signed on loan from Port Vale and he played seven games. Regular goalkeeper Gary Pierce then recovered from injury and played 27 games before injury put him out and Drew Brand was signed on a non-contract basis to play the final three games of the season.

A NEW STYLE REQUIRED

When Matt Gilks left the field after the 0-0 draw with West Ham United on 13 November 2010 no-one realised that he had a broken kneecap that was to keep him out of the side for some considerable time. He later said of the injury, "It fractured right across and broke in two bits. It was a little painful but it wasn't bad enough to make me want to come off. I hadn't realised it was broken." Two months down the line when he was resuming light training it became apparent that he had to adopt a new style of kicking to prevent a reoccurrence of the injury. He said, "We're going to address that and speak to some kicking coaches to see what they suggest. I kick with a very straight standing leg and all my power goes through it. Obviously that's what's caused the fracture and it's a factor in my injury."

FUNKY JAZZ

Early in the 1922/23 season the Great Harwood Jazz Band played at Bloomfield Road before home games. The band proved so popular that they were invited back for the game against Barnsley on 27 January 1923 when, to assist the club financially, a collection was made for the 'Shilling fund'. The slogan used to advertise the fund was "It costs you something to get into the First Division." And at the time Blackpool were well placed for promotion and by late March were at the top of the table. However, they fell away and finished a disappointing fifth.

HOME GROWN

When Blackpool defeated Preston St Joseph's 2-1 at Deepdale in the final of the Lancashire Junior Cup on 24 March 1888, ten of the players were born in Blackpool. Skipper George McVitie, Blackburn-born but moving to Blackpool when aged five, was the exception. The others were 'Lal' Wright, Tom Nelson, Harry Parr, Joe Schofield, 'Tishy' Hull, Tom Parr, Albert Bond, Joe Nelson, 'Little Billy' Parkinson and Billy Corry. Interestingly by 1924 all of the team, with the exception of Joe Nelson, who had died, were still living in Blackpool.

EASTER BONANZA

On Good Friday 1930 a new attendance record was created at Bloomfield Road when 23,868, who paid a record £1,825, watched Oldham Athletic defeated 3-0. Thousands invaded the pitch when the gates were stampeded so the quoted attendance was probably less than were actually in the ground.

SMART ADVERTISING

As well as the normal posters advertising the game against Small Heath at Raikes Hall on 27 October 1900, a striking handbill was issued to promote the game. It proclaimed, "Great Battle at Raikes Hall on Saturday when Blackpool, who are as yet undefeated, will meet Small Heath to settle who shall be premier club in the Second Division. If Lord Roberts [who was in South Africa in charge of troops fighting in the second Boer War] had only arrived in England we should have asked him to kick off at three o'clock." A "good" attendance was present to see the game drawn 0-0.

CHEEKY REQUEST

Preston North End paid Blackpool a high compliment when on 24 March 1900 they asked to borrow Bob Birket, Jack Morris, John Leadbetter and Harry Stirzaker for the remainder of the season in order "to get them out of the last two". For this they were prepared to pay Blackpool a substantial sum, transfer four of their league players to the club and pay the difference in their wages. Blackpool were not interested in any such deal and in the event Preston were relegated, finishing next to bottom of Division One.

DON'T BLAME THE PITCH!

Keith Wadeson, the groundsman at Bloomfield Road at the start of the 1999/2000 season, commented on his job, "The weather is all part of the job. It wouldn't be the same if the weather was glorious all the time and it certainly makes it more interesting for me. And I don't get too worried about not being the centre of attention. I just get on with my job and make sure the pitch is in the best possible condition." He continued, "I've been into football since I was eight years old when my uncle took me to see the Manchester derby at Maine Road. But I'm a Sandgrown'un, Blackpool born and bred, and I started supporting the Seasiders when I was about 12 – so getting the position as head groundsman at Bloomfield Road was superb for me. When I came here eight years ago to start work I was quite impressed with the pitch. It drains well and it doesn't cut up badly. In the eight years I've been here I've seen some great players and some great matches. I suppose the best match I've seen here was around four seasons ago when Blackpool played Chelsea in the old Coca-Cola Cup." He also commented, "The team now are a bit up and down. The lads have got to dig in and do their best to play ourselves out of the relegation zone." "But," he added, "one thing's for certain – you can't blame the pitch!"

UNFRIENDLY FRIENDLY

On the way back from playing a league game against Woolwich Arsenal Blackpool played a friendly game at Luton Town on 21 December 1896. They were defeated by non-league Luton Town 10-2 to receive "one of their biggest slatings known since they were a club" as they were "manifestly outmanoeuvred throughout". Luton scored five in each half and Blackpool replied with goals from Jack Parkinson and Nicholas Gillett.

GENEROUS HOSTS

Blackpool were on an eight-game winning streak when they visited Bury's Gigg Lane on 1 January 1937. They duly improved their record to nine games with a 3-2 win after which the host club presented Blackpool with a huge box of black puddings festooned in tangerine ribbons!

A HIGH-SCORING DRAW

Blackpool played a friendly game against Hull City on 28 January 1956 and the game was drawn 5-5. Blackpool's goals came from Jackie Mudie, four, and Bill Perry while Kenny Booth, in his initial game in the first team, "showed promise as a tricky inside-forward". Stan Mortensen, who scored two of Hull's goals, was "the brains of Hull's attack".

IN LOVING MEMORY

Over 200 Seasiders' supporters paid three shillings and ninepence [38p] for an excursion to Sheffield for a second round FA Cup tie in January 1906 and when they arrived at their destination they were greeted by supporters of First Division Sheffield United who were dispensing 'In Memoriam' cards which were to celebrate Blackpool's demise. In the event, Blackpool upset their plans and won 2-1 and at the end of the game supporters had a surprise in store for their Sheffield counterparts as they, too, had 'In Memoriam' cards. The card read In Loving Memory of UNITED/Gone the shout of din and rattle,/Gone our chances evermore,/Though it's been a glorious battle/The likes of which ne'er seen before./But the best team's won, I'm thinking,/So let's praise them all we can,/To their health let's all be drinking/Here's success to every man." The Blackpool players and officials were treated to a box seat at The Palace in recognition of their triumph.

MOVE ALONG PLEASE

Loudspeakers, which had been presented by the Blackpool Football Club Supporters' Club, were installed at Bloomfield Road prior to the opening game of the 1947/48 season. They were used for the first time for the game against Chelsea on 23 August 1947 when a new system of controlling the crowd allowed onto the terraces and embankments was put into operation. The intention was to usher spectators from one turnstile to another as the ground filled up and allowed the 48 turnstiles to have an allotted number of entries. Once that number had been reached the turnstile would close and spectators would move on to another one. The result was seen as "backwards and forwards from Bloomfield Road to Henry Street as the shutters went up the people surged"! A crowd of 27,389 saw Blackpool win 3-0.

IRISH EYES WEREN'T SMILING

Blackpool went on a pre-season tour of Ireland in August 1961 when two games were played. Distillery were beaten 5-1 on 11 August and Portadown were beaten 2-0 on the following day. Ray Parry, three, Brian Peterson and Dave Durie scored in the first game while Parry and Des Horne were on target in the second. Full-back Tommy Thompson, a former Great Britain Olympic Games player, was in the Blackpool party on trial and was "particularly impressive" while Stan Matthews limped off injured after 17 minutes of the Portadown game and was thereafter to play only two further first-team games for Blackpool before his move back to Stoke City.

MELANCHOLIA

When Blackpool lost 6-0 to Woolwich Arsenal on 18 March 1899 'PAT' in the *Morning Leader* was scathing about the team's performance. He wrote, "During the past few seasons I have been present at some melancholy football matches, but Saturday's was about the most mournful affair I have had the ill-luck to witness. From the start to finish there were not half a dozen occasions when Blackpool looked like scoring, and never looked anything like but easy losers, for their attacks, infrequent as they were, seldom lasted more than a few seconds. Even allowing for their 227 miles' trip, the Blackpoolians [sic] display was hard to account for. At home they had created some surprise lately, but on Saturday's form they were streets below what our own reserves can do, and were far from a testimonial to Second League class. Indeed, such mediocrity is seldom seen at Plumstead. Still I would counsel the Reds not to try the cat and mouse game at Blackpool the day after tomorrow, or they may be made to look very foolish. By going all the time they ought to add two more points to their present total of 34." Three days later Blackpool obviously improved for on 22 March the return game at Raikes Hall ended in a 1-1 draw.

A TALE OF A DUCK

The Atomic Boys acquired a new duck mascot named Puskas for the 1954/55 season and at Christmas 1954 the duck was exceptionally inaugurated into the Tailwaggers Club, a club previously reserved for dogs!

A GIANT SPONSOR

'Kickers-off' were an early type of sponsor at Blackpool and the person employed to kick off the game paid five pounds for the privilege. Against Barnsley on 15 March 1899 "The kicking-off ceremony was performed by a giant named Albert Brough, said to be the tallest man on earth and who stands seven foot five and a half inches." After he had set the ball rolling, "he dodged off the field in a wary manner and only seemed safe when he got to the stand". Some wag in the crowd commented, "Aye, if only he could play football. What a bonnie goalkeeper he would make."

BITTER-SWEET

When Blackpool defeated Tranmere Rovers 1-0 in the final of the Lancashire FA Youth Cup at Bloomfield Road on 3 May 1999 it was a bitter-sweet experience for goalscorer Ian Dickinson. The 17-year-old had learned just four days prior to the final that the club was releasing him. He commented, "It's great to score the winning goal in a cup final. It's just a pity I'm not here next year. I am happy with my goal but sad to be leaving."

MID-WEEK CHAMPIONS

The Lancashire Mid-Week League was formed in August 1922 with Blackpool's view being that it proved a very useful medium for giving trials to junior players. Blackpool won the title in 1925/26 when captain Reg Wright received the championship cup from league secretary Mr E Norman of Blackburn Rovers.

MILITARY HONOURS

Full-back or centre-half Johnny Crosland served as a pilot with the Fleet Air Arm in the Far East during World War II and he won the Distinguished Flying Cross, which was awarded for "an act or acts of valour, courage or devotion to duty whilst flying in active operations against the enemy". Injury to left-back Ron Suart gave Crosland the chance to play against Manchester United at Wembley in the 1948 FA Cup Final after having played only eight league games over a two-season period. Although Blackpool lost 4-2 he performed very creditably.

TWO REFEREES

When Blackpool played Black Lane Temperance at Bloomfield Road in the qualifying round of the FA Cup on 4 October 1902 the referee, Mr Lewis, was 20 minutes late in arriving. It was thought to be most unusual for him for he was deemed "one of the most methodical of men". A local referee took charge for the opening 20 minutes until Mr Lewis arrived and the pair of them saw Blackpool win 4-1.

THE TRAIN NOW DEPARTING ...

Blackpool were fined one guinea [£1.05] at a Football League meeting in Derby on 27 February 1903 for being late at Glossop on 17 February because they missed their connecting train at Manchester. Ironically one of the linesmen at the game, Mr F J Broughton, was also fined half a guinea as he missed the same train! To add insult to injury, Blackpool lost 1-0.

POPULAR LEICESTER

In two successive seasons Leicester City created a new attendance record at Bloomfield Road; 30,759 were present on Boxing Day 1936 to see Blackpool win 6-2 while 31,783 saw Leicester win 4-2 on 18 September 1937.

HIGH HOPES

The Blackpool directors thought that the overdraft that the club had accrued would be wiped out with a good FA Cup run in the 1913/14 season. And when the draw paired them with Southern League club Gillingham everything looked rosy. Sadly Blackpool lost 1-0 to the club that was ninth from the bottom of the Southern League.

FRENCH LEAVE

Team-mates Tony Waiters and Graham Oates met up in night school classes when both were taking a conversational French course at Claremont School in November 1963. Graham commented, "I'm off to France for my fourth annual holiday next year. I took book French in the GCE, but conversational French is much more useful." We all say, "Oui" to that!

A COSTLY ERROR

A newspaper headline reading Programme Number Comedy appeared following Blackpool's game with Leicester City on 18 September 1937. Every week two free centre stand tickets were given away to the holder of a lucky number that appeared on the programme. This week the winning number was 1000 and within minutes of the game ending about a dozen people made claim. Thinking that the error was only a small one the club generously honoured the commitment and gave away 12 sets of tickets. However, when the numbers of people with programme number 1000 swelled to hundreds, the club drew the line and said "no more". Over 800 people signed their programmes and left their addresses at the ticket office and it would have cost the club well over £250 to honour them all so no action was taken. Secretary Mr E G Crabtree stated, "Owing to a mistake made by the printers, which is explained by them as being due to the fact that the machine which registers consecutive numbers on the programme jammed, the number 1000 appeared for a large number of programmes which were sold." Blackpool's decision to stop issuing tickets resulted in a statement from the printer which was to the effect they "desire to express to the public their sincere regret for what has occurred, and trust that no inconvenience or annoyance will have been caused to any disappointed purchaser of a programme bearing the number 1000".

SCOTSMEN ALL

Against Chelsea at Bloomfield Road on 8 October 1938 Blackpool fielded an all-Scottish forward line in Alec Munro, Willie Buchan, Bobby Finan, Frank O'Donnell and Ken Dawson. They won 5-1 with Buchan scoring twice and O'Donnell netting a hat-trick, the first by a Blackpool player since Tom Jones scored four against Nottingham Forest on 28 November 1936.

DUTCH TREAT

Blackpool played Dutch First Division club Sparta Rotterdam in a preseason friendly game in Holland on 14 August 1957. A crowd of 25,000 saw goals from Ernie Taylor, Jackie Mudie and Bill Perry give Blackpool a 3-2 victory. Assistant secretary Fred Jones commented, "It was a fine match enjoyed by all in spite of some rain."

ILLEGAL SUBSTITUTION

In a Lancashire Senior Cup tie against Blackburn Rovers on 30 September 1901, Jack Parkinson, who was not playing due to injury, ran one of the lines in the first half. Goalkeeper Joe Dorrington took over for the second half but "as soon as the referee saw who the new linesman was, he reminded the officials that 'Dorrie' was under suspension" and another substitute linesman was found.

SARTORIAL ELEGANCE?

Following Blackpool's 1-0 defeat at Ewood Park by Blackburn Rovers in the FA Cup fourth round on 7 March 1925 a question was posed about the Blackpool colours "Tangerine and black. Are they the best colours for Blackpool?" The follow-up comment was "Tangerine and black may sound well, but the team cut a sorry figure at Ewood Park by comparison with the spotless and debonair blue and white of the Rovers." The criticism continued, "The black shorts of the Blackpool team were more greenish than black, and the general effect was dingy. They looked only half the size of the Rovers, largely because the sombre shades dwarf the players, while the speckless white shorts of their opponents showed them up to advantage." It was even asked, "Is Puddefoot's ability to bang the ball out to the wings with astonishing speed and accuracy possible mainly because he sees the bright patch of white out of the corner of his eye, while Bedford has to pause to find a figure which is largely camouflaged?" The conclusion was "At any rate, the moral effect of white is considerable, apart from the point of view of visibility. It is sheer foolishness to give away advantage before the game starts." The argument was supported by a comment at the game that was "There seems to be more Rovers men on the field than Blackpool," to which someone later replied "It was not altogether the speed of the winners that created this illusion. Some of it was due to the fact that one could see the Rovers through half-closed eyes, while the Blackpool men were just a dark blur." A final point was made by one far-seeing supporter who suggested a change of colour with "tangerine and white as the colours or, better still, white shorts with shirts of tangerine and black stripes" because, he felt, "Then they would look like the team they are – clever, alert and nippy, with a sting in the tail!"

MAD HATTERS

With Blackpool surging towards the First Division they were favourites to win their third round FA Cup tie against Division Three (South) Luton Town at Kenilworth Road on 16 January 1937. Sure enough Blackpool were leading 3-1 with goals from Bobby Finan, Dickie Watmough and Jack Middleton with five minutes remaining and Luton down to ten men. But the Hatters fought back to force a 3-3 draw. They came to Bloomfield Road for the replay on 20 January when the forecast was they would be "butchered on half day closing" but they confounded the critics by winning 2-1.

A FOUR-FIGURE TRANSFER

Blackpool received their record transfer fee to that date when full-back Charlie Gladwin was sold to Sunderland for a fee of £1,200 on 8 October 1912. However, the transfer came as "a very unpleasant shock to the supporters of the club" and prompted the following comment in the local press, "The most sensational occurrence in local football circles is the transfer of Charlie Gladwin to Sunderland, which will no doubt be talked about all over the country, for during the last few seasons more than one first-class club have been desirous of securing his services. The sum, topping four figures, is a record for the club, the previous highest being £750 for Bob Whittingham. Blackpool paid £10 for Gladwin from Dinnington Main, a mining district in the Midlands. He had improved wonderfully and there is much criticism in the club letting him go but it keeps the club out of financial difficulties, but if the club could persuade R H Gaskell, who played some storming games with the reserves last year, to play regularly, Gladwin's departure may not prove such a loss after all."

INS AND OUTS

Over nine months from August 1938 to April 1939 Blackpool were engaged in a succession of two-way transfer deals the like of which the club had never previously experienced. In that period £30,000 was spent and £19,750 recouped. The players signed were 'Jock' Dodds, £10,000, Dai Astley, £7,500, George Eastham, £5,000, Tommy Lewis, £5,000, and Hugh O'Donnell, £2,500, while those who were transferred were Frank O'Donnell, £10,500, Louis Cardwell, £6,000, Tom Jones, £2,000, and Tommy Lyon, £1,250.

COME RAIN OR SHINE ...

"What I would like to see one day is a cover over the Bloomfield Road Spion Kop. The fans who go there are with us in hail, rain and shine and they deserve all the comfort we can give them." So said manager Joe Smith at Blackpool's annual general meeting in August 1954. But it was not until Monday 25 April 1960 that a small army of workmen, cranes, piledrivers and concrete mixers invaded Bloomfield Road to begin work on covering two-thirds of the Kop. And there was an immediate problem – how deep they needed to drive the piles for the four supports of the roof. Deputy borough surveyor Mr D J Bell explained the problem: "An old map shows a dyke ran from Bloomfield Road in a northerly direction, and just to the east of where the football ground now is. Another dyke ran from west to east under what is now Rigby Road car park, and the two dykes met under what is now the rear of Field Street, which is just to the north-east of the ground. It is not surprising, therefore, that the ground underneath Bloomfield Road is so boggy." The club's assistant secretary Fred Jones commented, "It could be that they will have to go a really great depth before they come across firm ground. That has been the main problem whenever ground improvements have been carried out. It is expensive, too. A tremendous amount of money already has been spent on underground work – for the east paddock and the floodlights – which the public cannot see and so cannot appreciate. This is one of the financial problems that will have to be considered whenever the scheme for a new west stand is started." The work on the Spion Kop was to cost £17,000 and the roof would provide cover for around 11,000 spectators and when completed the ground would be one of the few in the country to provide covered accommodation on all four sides.

A TITLE LOST

The wartime season of 1939/40 saw Blackpool well placed in the North-West Regional League table and with three games remaining the club needed just three points to secure the title. However a 3-3 draw with Rochdale and 3-1 defeats by Carlisle United and Oldham Athletic saw them finish in a disappointing third place.

BLACKPOOL ENTERTAIN BOLTON WANDERERS ON A SNOW-COVERED PITCH ON 17 FEBRUARY 1940 WHEN BLACKPOOL WON 2-1.

NO MALINGERERS

A clause was inserted into the players' contracts for the 1946/47 season that stated there would be a cessation of first-team pay after four weeks' injury. The clause was inserted "to prevent malingering" and a notice to this effect was posted in the home dressing room!

JUDICIOUS APPOINTMENT

There was a short list of applicants for the manager's job in July 1935 when Messrs A Barritt, J Smith, J Thompson and P Travers made it to the last four. After interviews Joe Smith was appointed with a contract to run from 12 August 1935 to 3 May 1938 at a salary of £750 per annum. There was also to be a merit bonus of £500 if Blackpool gained promotion to the First Division, £250 if they were FA Cup semi-finalists and another £250 if they reached the FA Cup final. Smith remained in charge until 1958.

A WORTHY CAUSE

Blackpool played George Wilson's International XI on 10 May 1924 with the proceeds going to Lady Parkinson's appeal on behalf of the [Victoria] Hospital Bazaar Fund. The match, at Bloomfield Road, ended in a 3-2 victory for the International XI for whom Blackpool's Jack Meredith, a late call-up to the side, scored two goals, including the winner. All the players were presented with a silver cigarette case after the game.

ASHES WHITEWASH

On their tour of Australia in 1958 Blackpool played five 'Test' matches against the Australian national side and won them all. Not only did they defeat Australia on each occasion but they also scored 25 goals and conceded only six. The scores were 5-2, 8-2, 4-2, 1-0 and 7-0.

LIFE MEMBER

The first life member of Blackpool Football Club was Mr Eli Percival who was elected in August 1929 "in recognition of his services and handsome gifts to the club".

DEAL OR NO DEAL

"Stubbs is a good player but there is a limit to how high one can go. We are definitely not interested in him at the figure Torquay are quoting. If we are to re-open negotiations, they will have to lower their valuation. We would still be interested – but at the price we offered." So said Blackpool manager Ronnie Suart after his bid to sign Robin Stubbs, the league's leading goalscorer with 30 goals, failed in February 1965. Suart was so certain that he would get his man that a place had been left in the Blackpool side to play Leicester City on 13 February but, after a 360-mile round trip, the deal fell through in a Gloucester hotel. The stumbling block was the agreement that Torquay had with Birmingham City that they would pay the Midlands club half of any profit made on a future transfer. Torquay had paid Birmingham £6,000 and Blackpool had offered £25,000. But Torquay wanted £30,000 so that after paying Birmingham they would have been left with a £12,000 profit. A disappointed Suart added, "When I spoke to Mr Webber, Torquay's manager, on the phone I got the impression that my offer would be acceptable. Then I spoke to Mr Boyce and he mentioned a higher figure. I thought that if we could get together we could thrash it out so I suggested a meeting place halfway between Blackpool and Torquay and set off immediately for Gloucester." Stubbs was also disappointed and said, "Blackpool are a good club and I would have liked to join them." In the event Stubbs scored 120 goals in 217 games for Torquay before moving in July 1969 to Bristol Rovers where he wasn't as successful with 32 goals in 93 appearances.

LIGHTWEIGHT

When Preston North End accepted an invitation to play Blackpool in the Victoria Hospital Cup game on 8 May 1935, the club commissioned a series of medals for the occasion. They received quotes of 39 shillings [£1.90] from The Usher Manufacturing Co and of 40 shillings [£2.00] from Fatterini & Son but the directors thought the cost was too much for such an occasion and commissioned a medal of less weight. Fatterini & Son were eventually given the contract to produce the medals at a cost of 35 shillings each [£1.75].

ROYALLY ENTERTAINED

Following an historic FA cup second round victory over First Division Sheffield United in January 1906, the Blackpool players were all entertained in a box at The Palace theatre on 8 January. As well as the variety show, Robert Parkinson, a former Blackpool player, "in football costume, gave as an extra turn some excellent tenor songs". At the close of the production the Bioscope gave a picture of Blackpool's team plus individual photographs of Tommy Barcroft, the secretary, Bob Birket, the club captain, Harry Hancock, who scored the two goals at Sheffield, and Jack Scott, who captained the side in Birket's absence, to each of the patrons.

"I CLAIM THE £10"

The magazine *Pearsons* sent a £10 man to the Blackpool versus Burnley game on 8 December 1900 and any member of the crowd who spotted him could approach him and claim the £10 reward. Despite great efforts on everyone's part in the 3,500 crowd, including certain members of the clergy, the *Pearsons* man was not spotted.

ON THE SPOT

The Football Association introduced the penalty kick into the FA Cup competition for the 1891/92 season and Blackpool gained their first penalty in their final qualifying round match with Newton Heath. It was won when "Clements crossed over and deliberately tripped 'Gyp' Cookson" who was "within the limit". With seven minutes remaining, Harry Tyrer stepped up, took the kick and scored to give Blackpool a 4-3 victory.

NO DISPENSATION

Blackpool players Billy Park, Malcolm McLaren, Stan Franklin, Harry Johnston, George McFarland, Ken Edwards and Bill Theurer were coming of National Service age in the 1938/39 and 1939/40 seasons. Blackpool therefore wrote to the Ministry of Labour to see whether their six-month training in the armed forces could be split into two periods of three months each thus avoiding the football season and allowing the players to continue to play for the club. The Ministry of Labour would have none of it.

FANS' MAGAZINE

Blackpool Soccer Fan was a short-lived magazine that was published in the 1949/50 season. In the first number the editor stated, "I must make it clear at the outset that this publication has no official connection with Blackpool FC. Being independent of the club, we shall be free to praise, free to criticise … Articles by experts, photographs with artistic and action appeal, personal items about the players – those will be the ingredients of a magazine which we believe strikes a new note in sporting journalism." Unfortunately the magazine folded after five issues.

GOALLESS

Centre-half Roy Gratrix has a unique place in Blackpool history in that he played 436 league and cup games for the club between 1954 and 1964 and never scored a single goal. The nearest he came was when he took a penalty against Manchester City on 19 October 1957 but he "shot high over the bar".

TABLE TOPPERS

Blackpool opened the 1900/01 season with an 11-game unbeaten run and after ten of those games they went to the top of the Division Two table with five wins and five draws. They were ahead of Grimsby Town on goal average. Grimsby Town maintained their form to become champions but Blackpool sadly fell away to finish in 12th place.

CROWD PULLERS

When Blackpool played Workington on 25 November 1957 to celebrate the switching on of the club's floodlights a crowd of 16,000, by far the largest home gate for years, watched the game. Blackpool played a full-strength team and Bill Perry opened the scoring but Workington struck back with goals from Chisholm, Punlon and Robson, two, to win the game 4-1. Stan Matthews had to retire at half-time and was replaced by Ray Charnley. Matthews commented on his thigh, which had been strained at Birmingham the previous Saturday, "I had the impression that if I went full out it would give" and he missed the following two league games.

THE LILYWHITES

Blackpool were always said to look smart in their tangerine shirts, with white collars and cuffs and white shorts but when the continental style strip arrived in the late 1950s, Blackpool seemed to lose some of their smartness. Because of the colour clash at Turf Moor on 29 October 1960, Blackpool played in their change strip of all white, with tangerine collars and cuffs to the shirts and all white stockings with tangerine tops. Manager Ronnie Suart commented, "All white always does look very smart, and I must say the Blackpool team somehow look better in their change strip." Skipper Jimmy Kelly added, "I have heard quite a few comments about how good we looked last week. I prefer the all-white strip, and so do most of the lads, I think," while Stan Matthews said, "Playing in the all-white strip with tangerine flashings seems to give us a lift. I would rather have it than our usual strip." The change worked wonders as Blackpool defeated the reigning champions 2-1 with goals from Dave Durie and Bill Perry.

PLAY UP THE 'POOL!

Play up the 'Pool! was a "grand new football song" that was written and performed by Bertini and his Tower Band in February 1933. The proceeds of the sales of the music, price threepence, went to the Mayor's Fund for the Unemployed. It went on sale on 4 February 1933.

OFF-WHITE

A white ball was used in the pre-season practice game at Bloomfield Road on 13 August 1927 but it was deemed not to be a success. Several of the first-team players, when asked in the dressing room after the game, stated that they disapproved of the innovation. And trainer Albert Tulloch definitely considered the experiment to be a failure. The press view was "The ball did not seem exactly white at the start, but it almost resembled the ordinary ball at the end of the game. And this on a dry ground! From the spectators' point of view the white ball could not be said to be a success, because after it had been used for a little while it became grey in appearance, and was not so easy to follow during play."

SPEND A PENNY

The Blackpool Supporters' Club introduced a 'Penny on the Ball' scheme to raise money for the 1929/30 season. It was quite a success but the directors ordered it to be stopped prior to the 1930/31 season. The supporters' club appealed against the decision in September 1930 but the Blackpool board stood firm and confirmed their decision.

ADVENTUROUS PUBLICAN

For the Fylde Cup semi-final against South Shore on 22 December 1888 Mr Schofield of the Fleece Hotel, Blackpool produced a card with the legend 'Play up Blackpool' and they were "plentiful on the Waterloo ground" of South Shore. The *Blackpool Herald* commented, "Mr Schofield made a rare hit when he got those cards. They are excellent photos taken as a whole." Blackpool, the holders of the Fylde Cup, lost 1-0.

POINT(ER) LOST

In the summer of 1954 Blackpool gave a trial to a young centre forward who had been spotted playing for a local team in his native village of Cramlington in Northumberland. Ray Pointer came to the club for a month's trial at the end of which he was sent back to the north east. He commented, "At the end of the month I went back home and waited to hear from Blackpool but nothing happened." Pointer went on to join Burnley, after being spotted playing for Dudley Welfare, and won three caps for England. Ironically, after a career of over 400 games with Burnley, Bury, Coventry City and Portsmouth, Blackpool signed him, primarily to join the coaching staff for the 1973/74 season. He did, however, make sporadic appearances for the reserve and 'A' sides.

ALL SCOTS

When Blackpool signed Tom Lyon from Albion Rovers in March 1937 it meant that the club could field an all-Scottish eleven. The team would have been Jock Wallace, Danny Blair, Phil Watson, Frank Hill, Bob Dougal, G H Preston, Alec Munro, Lyon, Bobby Finan, Jimmy McIntosh and Willie Cook.

FOURTH ESTATE FACILITIES

When Blackpool visited Newcastle United's St James's Park for the third round FA Cup tie on 24 February 1906 the *Blackpool Times* correspondent felt fit to write, "The Press have a separate room, or balcony, over the centre stand, where they are enabled to report the games in comfort, even in the most wretched weather. I only wish Blackpool would devote a little of the surplus cash from Newcastle to making the Press accommodation at Bloomfield Road more becoming of a Second Division club, at present it is little short of a disgrace, as Pressmen do their work under the most disadvantageous conditions." From St James' Park the correspondent had to report a 3-0 defeat.

TWO NUMBER ONES

Blackpool played two goalkeepers in the game against Small Heath on 28 March 1903 when the press reported on "the astonishing novelty of a goalkeeper playing at outside-right". For some reason inside-left Fred Heywood, who played in every other game during the season, was not with the party that left for Birmingham. Fortunately Blackpool picked up reserve goalkeeper Joe Dorrington at Preston and he eventually played in goal with the regular goalkeeper Arthur Hull playing at outside-right. Perhaps not surprisingly Blackpool lost the game 5-1.

PREMATURE CELEBRATION

GOING UP! was the *Gazette* headline on 20 March 1924 followed by "Heading for the First Division", which came after Blackpool had defeated Port Vale 6-2. The supporting report went on to say, "It's a carnival. Nine more matches like that and we'll be halfway up the First Division league table, let alone being on top of the Second Division." The following game, the return with Port Vale, further strengthened the promotion view when Blackpool won 6-1. There was favourable comparison with the previous season when 'Pool had finished fifth, four points from a promotion place but the view was on this occasion "There is a vast difference in our favour. The team is game for a fighting finish and is not going to crack up as it did last season." Fatal words as Blackpool won only three of their final eight games and with three draws they finished in fourth spot, two points away from promotion.

A TOWN AMBASSADOR

Blackpool Football Club requested a £1,000 grant from Blackpool Town Council in October 1933 but the council awarded them only £500. Even so, Alderman Tom Bickerstaffe commented, "The Council realise that the football matches attract a lot of people to Blackpool. In many cases the visiting clubs run special trains, and other people besides the supporters of the team take the opportunity of spending a day in Blackpool."

FAR EASTERN DELIGHT

In October 1981 it was discovered that Blackpool had a Far East Supporters' Club that was the brainchild of Blackpool supporter Richard Dougal who was living in Singapore. Television in Singapore showed the highlights of one game on a Sunday morning sports programme each week and on 20 September 1981 it was Blackpool's 2-2 draw with Darlington. Dougal wrote to the *Gazette* stating, "As an ardent Blackpool fan for 34 years and self-appointed President of a small but flourishing Far East Fan Club, you can imagine my surprise and delight when, incredibly, the chosen match was Darlington v Blackpool. I would like Allan Brown and the players to know that Blackpool's two goals were heartily cheered here in Singapore, 8,000 miles from Bloomfield Road and that the club's encouraging start to the season is being followed closely and enthusiastically here in the Far East."

QUICK-CHANGE ARTISTS

When Blackpool played Birmingham City in the FA Cup semi-final replay at Goodison Park on 15 March 1951, they very nearly didn't arrive at the ground. The Blackpool coach was trapped in the Liverpool traffic and even the police could not help. The players eventually arrived at the ground just two minutes before the scheduled kick-off and they went into one of the fastest quick-change acts in football history. Outside 70,114 spectators waited patiently as Birmingham punted the ball about for a quarter of an hour and rumours in the ground were rife that Blackpool were not going to turn up. But, after pandemonium in the dressing room, they ran out, went into an early lead, never lost it and, winning 2-1, won a place in the cup final at Wembley for the second time in four seasons. And, also for the second time, they lost, 2-0 to Newcastle United.

SMOKING CONCERT

Blackpool Football Club held a 'Smoker', a smoking concert for gentlemen, at the Indian Lounge on 4 December 1900 to raise funds for the club and over 500 tickets were sold following the announcement "All who have the interests of the club at heart and wish for its advent into the First League should make a point of buying a ticket." Mr J J Bentley, president of the Football League, was the guest of honour and Councillor Bridge in welcoming him said, "It had been a great effort to keep football in the town in years gone by", adding that the town was pleased with the team's performance and stating the "paying powers of the club were the lowest of any club in either the First or Second Division so that the position they now occupied was very creditable indeed". Mr Bentley in reply stated that he had once played for Blackpool, was now married to a Blackpool lady and had something to do with the formation of the club that had gone through a variety of phases. He considered Blackpool "an exceedingly plucky club", felt the town would not be able to support First Division football as "the population was not large enough and First Division football was very expensive" and how he "could not believe Blackpool kept going at little over £12 per week" as other Second Division clubs were already paying out £40 to £50 per week. He finished by saying that he would not like Blackpool to gain promotion to the First Division as it would mean bankruptcy for the club.

COLOUR CLASH

In 12 of 21 away games in the 1937/38 season Blackpool had to change their strip from the light and dark blue stripes due to colour clashes. As a result the decision was taken to return to tangerine shirts for the 1938/39 season, the only difference being that the collars and cuffs were to be white instead of the previous black. The shorts would be white and the socks black with tangerine tops. Chairman William Parkinson stated, "We were disinclined to forsake the colours which my brother [previous chairman Sir Lindsay Parkinson] chose, but as this was more or less compelled, we came to the conclusion that the old tangerine was preferable to any colour for Blackpool."

A YOUNGER SIBLING

On 13 May 1933 Blackpool signed a 21-year-old amateur inside-left from Walkden Primitive Methodists in the Bolton League. He made his first, and what turned out to be his only, appearance for the Northern Mid-Week League side against Leeds United on 18 October 1933. He was named as Thompson but his resemblance to Blackpool's centre forward, Jimmy Hampson, was so remarkable that within minutes of the start the crowd were shouting "Come on, Jimmy"! As the game progressed the resemblance to Jimmy was not only confined to his appearance for he "revealed in glimpses, football precise and dapper", a definite footballing likeness to his brother. He scored one of the goals in a 3-3 draw and the strong rumour was that he was Fred Hampson, brother of Jimmy. Blackpool neither confirmed nor denied this but when Fred appeared for the Lancashire Amateur Association against the West Riding on 27 October 1934 reports stated he had "once been on trial with Blackpool but [was] not retained" and the story was repeated when he joined Hurst in November 1934. Interestingly no player by the name of Thompson or F Hampson appeared for Blackpool again that season.

LIES, DAMNED LIES AND STATISTICS

"There are three kinds of lies: lies, damned lies, and statistics," said 19th century politician Benjamin Disraeli. Well, there were plenty of statistics kept for Division Two clubs in the 1999/2000 season. For instance, Blackpool had 153 shots on target, 154 shots off target and two shots that hit the woodwork, categories that were led respectively by Gillingham with 269, Stoke City with 307 and Preston with 21. The Seasiders received 65 yellow cards and four red cards while leaders were Millwall and Reading both with 81 yellow and Cardiff City with seven red. The average home attendance was 4,840 with the highest attendance being the 9,042 who watched the game against Preston North End, who led the table with a home average of 12,818 with a highest attendance of 22,310 for their clash with Burnley. Blackpool's leading goalscorer was John Murphy with ten, Andy Payton of Burnley being the Division's top scorer with 27. And finally, as the season ended Blackpool had gone six games without keeping a clean sheet but were well behind the unenviable record of 14 that Chesterfield held.

TO BE OR NOT TO BE, A PUBLICAN

When Sheffield United placed a ban on any of their players keeping licensed premises it put an end to full-back Eddie Shimwell's career at Bramall Lane as he had just taken up the licence of The Plough Inn, Two Dales, near Matlock. Consequently he was transferred to Blackpool for a fee of £7,500 on 20 December 1946. He went on to play 319 games for the Seasiders and, appearing in three FA Cup finals, he was later to comment, "Pulling pints won me a cup medal."

SPOT ON

Of 111 penalties that were awarded in the Second Division in 1909/10 Blackpool had four, scoring from three of them. Manchester City topped the chart with ten, scoring from seven.

EARLY NICKNAME

When Blackpool played in blue and white stripes in the late 1880s and through to the 1890s they had the nickname 'The Merry Stripes'.

PLAY-OFF PREMIERS

When Blackpool defeated Cardiff City 3-2 at Wembley on 22 May 2010 they became the first team to win through to the top flight of English football from the basement by winning three play-off finals. They defeated Leyton Orient 4-2 at the Millennium Stadium to move from League Two to League One on 26 May 2001 and defeated Yeovil 2-0 at the same venue on 27 May 2007 to move from League One to the Championship before their Wembley triumph.

ENTHUSIASTIC SUPPORT

At a very well attended general meeting of the members of Blackpool Football Club on 24 August 1887 at the Stanley Arms Hotel the committee announced that they already had 30 vice-presidents, that the club was gaining "any amount of support" and that they confidently expected the forthcoming season would "eclipse all other ones".

EDDIE SHIMWELL WITH HIS WIFE AND SON OUTSIDE HIS HOSTELRY, THE PLOUGH INN.

FRIENDLY PERSUASION

When Blackpool had to seek re-election to the Football League after finishing bottom of Division Two in 1908/09 the club issued an appeal to other clubs in an effort to garner enough votes to be re-elected. The appeal read, "Our unfortunate position at the bottom of the Second Division renders it necessary for us to seek re-election. May we, therefore, place before you a brief statement of the affairs of the Club, trusting thereby to bid strongly and confidently for your kind support and vote. This is the first occasion we have had to apply since our election in 1899. Of the 38 League games played last season, we won 9, and drew 11; and of the games lost 7 of them were only by the odd goal. We mention this to show that although we finished last, we have produced football of a character that has not disparaged us in the eyes of our opponents or of their supporters. During the past year we spent upwards of £1,000 on improving our ground, new stands, dressing rooms etc. In anticipation of being successful at the poll, we are leaving no stone unturned to secure players of a calibre which we sincerely trust may worthily uphold the best traditions of present-day League football, both on and off the field. Notwithstanding that our wage list last season was £80 per week, we managed to defray the total cost of improvements out of revenue, and finish the season with a balance on the right side. We have been happy during past seasons to be of service to all League Clubs when making Blackpool and district their training quarters, to give them free use of the ground etc., and we shall be only too pleased to do so again in the future. In conclusion, we appeal to you as a club, perhaps not in the first flight, but which has always played strenuously and honourably for the best interests of the League and the game generally, and ask you from our lowly position to extend towards us the practical help you are able to give." The appeal had the desired effect, for at the meeting of the Football League in London on 8 June 1909 Blackpool were comfortably re-elected with 27 votes while Lincoln City, who had dropped out of the League previously in 1907/08, were the other club elected with 24 votes. Unsuccessful were Chesterfield Town, applying for immediate re-election, with 21 votes and Stoke City, who polled only six.

SUCCESS IN SCOTLAND

The pre-season of 1968/69 saw Blackpool embark on a short Scottish tour in which they played Partick Thistle on 29 July 1968, St Mirren on 1 August and Aberdeen on 3 August. Partick were beaten 4-1 with Alan Skirton scoring a hat-trick in 19 minutes and with another goal from John McPhee, St Mirren were beaten 5-2 with Skirton, two, Milne, Hutchison and Suddick on target and there was a 1-1 draw with Aberdeen when Gordon Milne scored. In all three games Blackpool played the same team, which was Alan Taylor, Jimmy Armfield, Henry Mowbray, Gordon Milne, Glyn James, John McPhee, Alan Skirton, Terry Alcock, Tony Green, Tom White, Alan Suddick and Tommy Hutchison. The only change was for the second half of the Aberdeen game when Gerry Ingram replaced an injured Hutchison.

BARGAIN BUY

The £7,000, £6,000 down and a further £1,000 after six league games, that Blackpool paid Tranmere Rovers for half back Johnny Green on 13 March 1959 was the most the club had laid out on a transfer for five years since the £15,000 paid to Watford for Jimmy Kelly in 1954. The modest transfer fee proved to be a real bargain as Green went on to play 147 league and cup games for the club over eight seasons, being an ever-present in the 1964/65 season.

LIVE ON AIR

History was made at Bloomfield Road on 14 October 1939 when the ground became a relay station for the BBC. In the first ever broadcast from the north-west coast Mr Tom Cragg, up in the press box on the back row of the west stand, gave second half commentary into a telephone from 4.15pm to 5.00pm. In the game Blackpool defeated Manchester United 6-4.

MANAGERLESS

From 1928/29 to 1932/33 Blackpool did not employ a manager for team affairs and a players & advisory committee, which reported to the full board of directors, handled selection.

VISITORS BEMUSED

When Blackpool lost their third round FA Cup tie 5-0 to Newcastle United at St James' Park on 24 February 1906 34,405 spectators were present, the largest crowd that had watched Blackpool play to that date. It was recorded as "the gate of a lifetime" and "Blackpool people simply stared with astonishment, and the officials' faces beamed with satisfaction." One contemporary report read, "The scene inside the enclosure will never be forgotten by the visitors. Most of them had never seen such a sea of faces. The Blackpool officials 'chuckled and laughed, aha!' when they rubbed between their fingers the crisp cheque for that amount [the Blackpool receipts were £521 4s 7d]. The defeat by five goals was not thought of."

BROTHERLY LOVE

Brothers John and Brian Butler switched roles once they joined Blackpool. Elder brother John was a midfield star when he moved from schools football but he was converted to full-back while Brian was a full-back who switched to midfield. Reserve coach Jack Chapman commented on John, "He has proved a ready convert from defence to midfield. He not only tackles well but his work rate is excellent." And manager Sam Ellis was pleased with both boys' progress.

FADED GLORY

Even though Blackpool's tangerine strip had been in use for two seasons, it still came in for some criticism even at the start of the 1925/26 season. Southampton were the visitors on opening day 29 August and one observer commented, "Their clean red and white striped shirts, uniform knickers and stockings were a delightful contrast to the faded marigold shirts and jumbled shorts and stockings of the home team." Warming to his subject he added, "At least, and especially now that we have so many women spectators, the team should have turned out in perfect attire for the first match." As for the goalkeeper's jersey he wrote, "Crompton's jersey was enough to make him nervous. It was any colour but that intended, and stood out prominently as a reminder that someone is lacking smartness." Despite their apparent rag, tag and bobtail outfits, Blackpool won the game 2-1 with goals from Harry Bedford and Jack Meredith.

PATHFINDERS

Before the start of the 1897/98 season a new kind of season ticket was issued to Blackpool supporters. They were to be published in book form with the name of the respective match plus the date printed on each page, eg 4 September Blackpool v Burnley. The idea was simple in that on entering the ground patrons would tear the respective page out of the book and hand it to the gateman. The club stated its purpose was to "do away with the practice of people dropping their tickets over the wall to a friend after they have entered the ground". The consensus of opinion was "It is a very good idea and other clubs would do well to follow."

TOO MUCH TO SAY

Goalkeeper Joe Dorrington was sent off against Burnley at Turf Moor on 13 April 1901. The incident was reported thus: "Dorrington was sent off the field for talking to the referee who had given a penalty against Blackpool, Dorrington protested against this course, but the referee was inexorable in spite of endeavours on the part of the Burnley men to cause him to alter his mind." Centre-half Harry Stirzaker went in goal and McLintock immediately beat him from the penalty spot. The same player added another penalty later in the game to make the score an emphatic 4-0 in Burnley's favour. The Blackpool correspondent reported, "It was too terrible for anything and after that one could hardly have been surprised if the homesters had beaten us by a dozen. Wasn't that ref partial? To Burnley! It's a bit thick when the benefiting team disagree with him, too. To order 'Dorrie' off the field was an outrage on the series of fair play."

FOUR YEARS IN THE PLANNING

The new South Stand erected at Bloomfield Road in 1926 replaced the original Spion Kop, which had been at the south end of the ground. On the erection of the new stand, the suggestion was made that the following season would see a scheme that would include "the changing of the goal areas and the building of a Spion Kop at the north end of the ground". In the event the new north end Spion Kop did not appear until 1930.

SURPRISE VICTORY

When Blackpool defeated Small Heath 3-2 on 29 January 1898 it came as something of a surprise because the players "rose at dawn of day. They journeyed to Birmingham, 'cribbed, cabined and confined' as the poets say, in a musty railway carriage; and then they tumbled out upon a football field with legs unstretched and the midday meal undigested." The critics' view was that Blackpool played above themselves and "the Birmingham fellows were rocky".

AN EARLY BATH

Alex Downie of Manchester United was sent off in the game at Bloomfield Road on 14 February 1903. He had been cautioned in the first half but in the second Anderson robbed him of the ball and he "ran after him, and deliberately kicked him on the leg from behind". "Without a moment's hesitation" the referee sent him off. His dismissal was the second of the game because a spectator was ordered from the ground by the referee at half-time. The Manchester spectators, who were "a disgraceful gang" throughout, had consistently hooted and chivvied the referee and at half-time one of the linesmen complained of the behaviour of one particular spectator. The (unbiased) referee, who happened to be the Blackpool secretary Mr R B Middleton, and a policeman went over to the front of the grandstand and removed the gentleman in question from the ground, "amid considerable excitement". As for the game, goals from Walter Cookson, a stunning overhead kick, and Ted Threlfall gave Blackpool a 2-0 victory.

IDENTIFIABLE STEWARDS

Leicester City visited Bloomfield Road on 18 September 1937 when 31,783 were present and the gates were closed. This situation usually caused problems in the ground but on this occasion the new stewards, recruited two weeks earlier by secretary Ed Crabtree, "packed the people on the terraces and in the paddocks so efficiently that there were no invasions of the playing areas and no encroachment over the barriers". The stewards were readily identifiable as they were all clad in bright yellow waterproofs.

AUTOCRATIC CONTROL

When manager Joe Smith was re-engaged for three years in May 1938 he was to have complete control of the training, coaching, ground and playing staff. For this he was to be rewarded with a salary of £750 per annum, plus an additional £500 if the club were to become First Division champions, £250 if they reached the FA Cup semi-final and £250 if they reached the FA Cup Final. However, the directors made it clear that they would review the terms if the club were relegated.

SPRINGBOKS TO THE FORE

Blackpool had four South Africans in their line-up against Tottenham Hotspur on 19 August 1961. Peter Hauser was at right-half, Des Horne at outside-right, Brian Peterson at inside-right and Bill Perry at outside left. Englishman Ray Charnley scored the consolation goal in a 2-1 defeat.

THINGS ONE WONDERS

The *Sheffield Sports Special* ran an article entitled "Things one wonders" in January 1923 and two of the queries were: "How do Blackpool carry on if gates of last Saturday's dimensions, 30 December, [10,000 watched Blackpool defeat Sheffield Wednesday 3-0] are the rule?" and "How did they manage to pay £1,500 for the transfer of Jimmy Wood from Huddersfield Town?" Needless to say, the questions were left unanswered.

A FOOTBALLING VICAR

The Reverend S Gamble-Walker of Victoria Congregational Church gave his second football service on Sunday 28 March 1909 and the subject of his sermon was 'The Penalty'. He opened with reference to Blackpool's performance the previous day when they had defeated Stockport County 2-1 and said the game was "one of the finest seen at the Bloomfield Road enclosure during the two seasons I have been in town". He then discussed the penalty kick, explaining its introduction into the game as "to protect any unfair advantage being taken of a player who was likely to give his side the lead". He later assured the congregation that the Blackpool players "donned the jersey not to kick an opponent but [to kick] the ball".

KNOCK DOWN PRICES

On Wednesday afternoon 27 December 1899, shortly after Blackpool had amalgamated with South Shore FC, Mr Hugh Ormond, the County Court bailiff, sold the grandstand, the pay-box and the hoardings of the South Shore club at Bloomfield Road. A Mr Hamilton bought the stand and hoardings for seven pounds ten shillings [£7.50] and a local farmer bought the pay-box as a hen house for 11 shillings and twopence [56p]!

IT'S TANGERINE NOT ORANGE

When Blackpool turned out at Bloomfield Road against Crystal Palace on 29 September 1923 "the Blackpool players appeared in jerseys of a new shade of tangerine. The new jerseys, not quite so heavy in texture as the others, looked smart with their black collars." One "rude person" who shouted, "Hello, here are the oranges," was removed from the ground!

A FINANCIAL LIFELINE

In January 1925 Blackpool Football Supporters' Club was formed following a crisis meeting held by the football club in the Free Library at which the tenuous financial position of the club was explained. After the meeting two or three hundred fans who were interested in forming a supporters' club met and with Mr Handel White as chairman began to work hard to wipe out the football club's £3,000 debt. They duly did so by the end of the 1925/26 season and had raised so much money that they planned to put some terracing on the popular, east, side of the ground and then put a cover over it. A ladies' committee, under the chairmanship of Miss L Furber and with Miss Gallagher as secretary, was formed to raise extra money for the purpose.

CHARITABLE FRIENDLY

On 6 May 1960 Blackpool Youth team met Preston North End Youth at Morecambe's ground in a friendly game that was in aid of the Lancaster YMCA Appeal Fund. Blackpool, with a team of West, Burrows, Cuthbert, Hartwell, Fillingham, Turner, Ogilvie, Watt, Napier, McGuigan and Tyrell lost the game 4-0.

SOUTHERN LEAGUE SPURS

Blackpool first met Tottenham Hotspur, then of the Southern League, in a friendly game at Northumberland Park on 21 November 1896 when, in front of 3,000 spectators, Blackpool won 2-0 with goals from Sam Donnelly and James Martin. Blackpool had departed for "the wilds of London" on Friday and arrived at their destination Ye Old Belle Hotel with "a desire for something to eat and a speedy exit for halldom – which is Piccadilly way". The players went west and "beyond shaking up the piano as the tinkler had never been shaken up before, and mixing certain bed equipments, they conducted themselves as footballers". They spent Sunday at St Paul's Cathedral and the Tower of London before catching the midnight train back to Blackpool.

FIRST DIVISION LEADERS

In a survey carried out up to the end of the 1997/98 season Blackpool had been at the top of Division One, ie ahead of all other clubs, for a total number of 136 days and the club ranked 26th of the 48 clubs that had topped the top flight table since 1888. The leaders of the chart, Liverpool, had topped the table for 3,246 days while last of the 48 was Carlisle United with just three days. Blackpool did lead the Premier League table in 2010/11 after their 4-0 opening day win over Wigan Athletic but the reign lasted only a few hours until Chelsea overtook them on goal difference.

REVENGE IS SWEET

After losing 4-2 to Manchester United in the FA Cup Final at Wembley on 24 April 1948, Blackpool played the same opponents in a league game at Bloomfield Road just four days later. Blackpool wanted to take revenge in front of their own supporters while United wanted to prove that their win was no fluke. In front of a crowd of 32,236 the game did not disappoint and it was a superb diving header from Stan Mortensen that won the points for Blackpool in the 1-0 victory. Unfortunately, later in the game 'Morty' collided with United goalkeeper Jack Crompton and had to be taken to hospital unconscious. Fortunately he made a rapid recovery and was able to take his place on England's close-season tour of the continent.

MISDEMEANOURS

The Blackpool directors suspended Lionel Watson and 'Yaggie' Read for a fortnight in January 1909 for "putting in only small percentages of attendance at the ground for training". The directors felt that the latitude they allowed the players was being taken advantage of and, therefore, they took action and issued the suspensions as examples to the others.

FINAL SCORE

A tobacconist's shop at the corner of Church Street and St Anne's Street, now the site of the Grand Theatre, and owned by a Mr Tommy Thompson, was a place where all the local football results were gathered in the mid-1880s. Mr Thompson "got all the earliest results" and "his shop became the rendezvous of football enthusiasts eager to get all the earliest information of the doings of clubs".

SNOW SHIFTERS

A gang of 50 men recruited from the Labour Exchange cleared the Bloomfield Road pitch of six inches of snow after starting at seven o'clock in the morning and with the fog that had shrouded the Fylde lifting, the referee declared the FA Cup third round tie against Sheffield United on 7 January 1939 playable just an hour before the kick-off. The match turned out to be as grim as the day as Blackpool lost 2-1 in front of a disappointing attendance of 15,000. Tom Lewis gave Blackpool the lead after 20 minutes but injured full-back Harry Hooper gamely headed United back on level terms after a cross by former Blackpool junior Harold Barton six minutes later. And then with eight minutes remaining Blackpool conceded the winning goal.

SEEING RED

Most unusually Blackpool played in red and white stripes, instead of their normal white shirts, in the FA Cup first round replay against Derby County on 14 January 1920 and also in the second round tie against Preston North End on 30 January 1920. Derby County were beaten 4-1 but Preston triumphed 2-1.

CATHKIN LIGHTS

Blackpool played part-timers Third Lanark to open the Cathkin Park floodlights on 30 November 1959. Blackpool played a full strength side and although Dave Durie scored the goal of the night as he "wiggled and swayed his way past three defenders" before putting an 18-yard shot into the net, Blackpool lost 3-2 to a late penalty. A crowd of 10,000 saw Blackpool overrun Third Lanark for ten minutes but thereafter the part-timers took over as Blackpool's forwards were often "running in the wrong direction".

A BOLD DECISION

Blackpool refused an offer of £600 to move the first round FA Cup tie against Derby County on 10 January 1920 to the Baseball Ground. Blackpool gambled that they would make more money playing the game at home and it went ahead at Bloomfield Road and was drawn 0-0 in front of a crowd of 11,000. The replay four days later attracted 20,000 and they saw goals from Joe Lane, two, Jack Sibbald and Jack Charles give Blackpool a 4-1 win over their First Division opponents.

HEADS OR TAILS?

The 1938 Victoria Hospital Cup was won by Blackpool, not on the Bloomfield Road ground but in the dining room of the Savoy Café. The game was drawn 2-2, Frank O'Donnell and George Farrow from a penalty scoring for Blackpool and Tommy Lawton and Jimmy Cunliffe replying for Everton, so a coin was tossed at the celebration dinner after the game and Blackpool called correctly. The money raised from the game took the total for such games since the inauguration of the competition in 1925 to £2,500.

TICKET TOUTS

Tickets for the visit of Manchester United on 14 November 1964 were on sale outside various entrances at Bloomfield Road. Ticket touts were asking 30 shillings [£1.50] for a six shillings and sixpence [33p] ticket because the game had become a sell-out a few days earlier. A crowd of 31,129 watched United win 2-1 with Denis Law being sent off, a decision that sparked scuffles on the Spion Kop among rival fans.

DON'T MOVE

In the first round of the Watney Cup on 29 July 1972 Blackpool drew 0-0 with Peterborough United in front of 7,651 spectators and the game went immediately to penalty kicks. After the statutory five penalties to each side the score was 4-4 and so the shoot-out went to sudden death. Both teams scored their first two to make it 6-6 and then Alan Ainscow hit a post. Peterborough's Frank Noble stepped up and put his penalty wide but the referee decided that Blackpool goalkeeper John Burridge had moved and ordered the kick to be retaken. It was, Noble scored and Peterborough were through 7-6.

A CHRISTMAS TREAT

Stan Mortensen once told a tale about how he played after a big Christmas dinner. He said, "I recall that one Christmas I came home on leave at short notice, and my relatives did me proud. I began with the first course and went right through the meal to the inevitable Christmas pudding. Then I strolled down to Bloomfield Road to, as I thought, watch the game. But I was spotted, and in next to no time the honeyed words of Mr Joe Smith persuaded me into a football shirt and shorts. To say that the first 20 minutes of that match was agony is understating the case. It was agony for me to run, and I am sure my team-mates, the manager and the spectators suffered too."

CELEBRITY FANS

In the late 1940s and early 1950s Blackpool had any number of celebrity fans such as bandleaders Geraldo, Ted Heath, and Henry Hall and Charlie Chester and Donald Peers, all of whom had performed summer seasons in the resort. In particular Geraldo, whose real name was Gerald Walcan Bright, would follow the club all over the country and prior to the 1948 FA Cup Final he turned up at the club's Ascot hotel the day before the game. The players had been playing cards, walking and listening to the radio to calm their nerves and to assist the process Geraldo entertained them to a brilliant impromptu piano recital that, for a short time, took the players' minds off the important game of the following day.

AWAY SUPPORT

When Port Vale brought 50 spectators to watch their team play Blackpool at the Athletic Grounds on 24 September 1898 it brought forth the comment in the *Blackpool Times*: "It is a long time since the Blackpool team commanded fifty followers on its journeys – especially when travelling such a distance."

BRIEF HOUR OF GLORY

When Blackpool transferred goalscoring centre forward Harry Bedford to Derby County in September 1925 they were worried where their next marksman would come from. Then they signed Albert Fishwick from Plymouth Argyle in October 1925 and although he did not score on his debut, he netted seven in his first six games and he finished his first season at the club as the leading goalscorer with 19 goals in 26 games. However, despite his ability to find the net regularly, he was in and out of the first team over the next two seasons and when he was transferred to Port Vale in April 1928 he had scored 36 goals in 57 games.

UNLUCKY THIRTEEN

The news on 10 March 1961 was sensational, "Blackpool to Transfer 13". Eight of the players were offered on a free transfer and they were Hughie Kelly, Malcolm Harding, Alan Burrows, Jack Fillingham, David Jones, David Demaine, Brian Tyrell and Frank McGuigan. The other five commanded a fee and they were Sammy Salt, Bruce Crawford, Les Campbell, Barrie Martin and Peter Smethurst. The decision to release the players came following the announcement of the proposed new wage structure for players that was to be introduced in the summer of 1961 and the Blackpool directors had the difficult task of deciding how many players they should keep. Manager Ronnie Suart commented, "The 13 players have been notified [early] in order to give them more time in which to find another club."

A FULL STAFF

Blackpool retained 40 players on the league list for the 1906/07 season but the club made it known "of course, there are a number of others open to transfer".

PSEUDONYMOUS

When outside-right Jack Charles died on 16 June 1960 it transpired that his real name was John William Chandler and that he had used 'Jack Charles' for professional purposes. Nobody at the club was aware of this even though he had been with Blackpool for 24 years as player and trainer.

FOND MEMORIES

When Blackpool drew Chester at home in the fourth round of the FA Cup in 1948, their manager Cecil Marsh was returning to a familiar stamping ground for he had been a Blackpool player for two seasons just after World War I. The Yorkshireman was signed from Sheffield United in May 1919 but he played only two league games while at Bloomfield Road although he was a member of the Central League championship-winning side of 1919/20. There was no joy on his return as the Seasiders won 4-0.

MOVE? NO, THANKS

In October 1937 Blackpool were approached by the Town Council and asked if the club would be prepared to sell the Bloomfield Road ground with the suggestion that a stadium be built for the club at the Oval in Stanley Park. Chairman Mr W Parkinson agreed with his board members that the club "could not consider removing to either Squires Gate or Stanley Park" and the unanimous view was that if the Corporation wanted to assist the club they could build an improved stadium on the Bloomfield Road site.

A TRAGIC END

Blackpool-born Jack Parkinson played 405 games for the club between 1896 and 1909 before moving to take over as manager of Barrow. He remained with Barrow for one season before returning to Blackpool to become manager of the Corporation baths in Cocker Street, starting his new job in autumn 1910. Sadly he was involved in a tragic accident at the baths after falling in a vat of boiling water when trying to rescue a colleague, engineer Isaac Howcroft, on 20 December 1911. The cause was "the collapse of a wooden platform over a large tank used for storing hot salt water required in the baths" and Parkinson died from his injuries two days later.

HORACE FAIRHURST, WHO TRAGICALLY DIED FOLLOWING A HEAD INJURY SUSTAINED IN THE GAME AGAINST BARNSLEY ON 27 DECEMBER 1921.

UNCOMFORTABLE JOURNEY

For the third game of the 1900/01 season, Blackpool left Talbot Road railway station at 8am and arrived at their destination, Walsall, five hours later! The London & North Western Company were unable to supply a saloon for the players to travel in and "the journey was not made as comfortable as the travellers wished". Any discomfort did not, however, hinder the team's progress on the pitch as goals from Bob Birket and Lorrie Evans gave the Seasiders a 2-1 victory that put them in sixth place in the table.

PLANS PUT ON HOLD

In April 1960 Blackpool planned to have a new west stand and needed 100 supporters to help financially. The 100 would get a season ticket, a comfortable seat commanding a good view of the pitch, a private boardroom and other facilities. "What we have in mind," said chairman Albert Hindley, "is the forming of a '100' club. The club would comprise 100 members each giving 90 guineas, plus ten guineas a year subscription to the parent club in return for the facilities. The money received would give us a good start in the building of a new stand. So anybody interested in the scheme would be helping us immensely if they would let the club know. Sufficient response could mean the success of the scheme." Aware that the ground needed modernising he added, "We envisage an enlarged concrete stand on the west side, giving patrons comfortable seats and ample leg room. Underneath could be housed dressing rooms, offices, club rooms and other accommodation. But all this will cost about £150,000 and will depend on the corporation's willingness to provide a loan for ground improvements and possibly on the response of the '100' club idea." A club was formed but it was to be another 40 years before the development of a new west stand.

AN ILL-FATED LOAN

Brian Quailey joined Blackpool on loan from West Bromwich Albion on 3 December 1999 and made his debut the following day in a 1-1 draw with Wrexham. However, he only played another 14 minutes for the club as he was injured in the Auto Windscreens Shield tie with Notts County on 7 December and had to leave the field. As a consequence he returned to West Bromwich Albion before his loan spell was due to end.

SECOND CHOICE

Jack Peart of Bradford was offered the manager's post at Blackpool in the summer of 1933 but he was unable to get his release from Bradford so Blackpool appointed Alec Macfarlane at a salary of £750 per annum. He was to receive a £500 bonus if the club reached the First Division and the same amount should they get to the FA Cup Final. He didn't earn either bonus but remained with the club until the end of the 1934/35 season.

GO WEST YOUNG MAN

"West Ham United has never shown itself a Cup tie team. I think they are cleverer than Blackpool, but good clubs have come a cropper at the Lancashire watering place. Added to this that the Hammers are at present a disappointing team, and it must be admitted that over-confidence should not be the policy of the East Londoners. If they can but draw at Blackpool, I shall not fear their chance in the replay," wrote a London newspaper correspondent after Blackpool had drawn West Ham United in the first round of the FA Cup in 1906/07. However, even as the words appeared in print the Blackpool committee was considering selling the ground rights and moving the game to London, "purely owing to the financial considerations". A Manchester newspaper got wind of the proposed change and in an editorial stated, "Blackpool ought to have a fair chance of beating West Ham ... it is hoped that the committee will not agree to change the venue of the Cup to the West Ham ground for a consideration ... it will take a very large bait to tempt them, especially with such a prospect of qualifying outright for the second round, or making a draw and then participating in a good gate at the Metropolis". The committee estimated costs of £150 at Bloomfield Road so, after an initial offer from West Ham was rejected, they agreed to move the game south for £150 plus half the gate receipts. In front of 13,000 (some reports varied between 12,000 and 20,000) Western League side West Ham won 2-1 but Blackpool did return home with £350 once expenses had been deducted. It was no consolation but one London newspaper reported, "The result would seem to suggest that if Blackpool had kept the match on their own ground they might have won."

A LITTLE DOGGEREL

After Blackpool had defeated South Shore 4-0 on 25 February 1893, a local poet penned the following lines, a pastiche on Fred Gilbert's 1892 music hall song The Man Who Broke the Bank at Monte Carlo, "As I walk along the Promenade with an independent air/You can hear the tarts declare, He must be a millionaire;/For I backed the stripes to beat the whites,/Drew the money from green Shoreites,/And I'm off to mend the bank in Monte Carlo."

FOUNDER MEMBERS

At a meeting in London on 26 May 1911 it was resolved "That the Lancashire clubs, members of the Lancashire Combination, resign from that Combination and form a new League, and that application be made to the Football Association for affiliation." A sub-committee was to be set up to make the necessary rules etc and that sub-committee met at the Imperial Hotel in Blackpool on 29 May 1911 and resolved "That the new League be called the Central League." There were 18 clubs, of which Blackpool was one and the new championship began on 2 September 1911 when Blackpool reserves defeated Burnley reserves 3-0 with two goals from Peter Quinn and one from Joe Bainbridge. Blackpool finished the first season in ninth place with a record of P32 W12 L12 D8 Goals for 43 Goals against 52 points 32.

ACROSS THE BOARD

Brett Ormerod became the first player to play for Blackpool in all four divisions of the Football League when he appeared against Wigan Athletic on 14 August 2010. He had played in League One and League Two in his first spell at the club and in the Championship and the Premier League in his second spell.

NO CHANGE

By the beginning of 1950 only five First Division clubs, Blackpool, Charlton Athletic, Liverpool, Sunderland and Stoke City, had the same manager as they had at the start of World War II. Blackpool's Joe Smith was to remain in charge at Bloomfield Road until 1958 when he retired due to ill health.

ONE A SEASON

Malcolm Starkey played just three league games for Blackpool but he had the unusual distinction of playing them over a three-season period at the rate of one per season. He made his debut at outside-left, replacing the injured Bill Perry, in a 3-2 victory over Wolverhampton Wanderers, Perry returned for the following game and so Starkey went back to reserve team football. His second appearance came on 4 April 1958 when he replaced the unavailable Dave Durie in a Good Friday game against Preston North End, who won 2-1. His final appearance was against Bolton Wanderers on 18 October 1958 when the forward line was shuffled and he appeared at inside-left in a 4-0 defeat. After five years at Bloomfield Road he was transferred to Shrewsbury Town on 8 June 1959 for a fee of £1,750. He also played for Chester before returning to Shrewsbury as a much-respected secretary, a post he held for almost 40 years before his retirement.

TAYLOR-MADE

Alan Taylor began his football as a centre-half, starring for Claremont School, but by the time he signed as an amateur for Blackpool in September 1962 he had become a goalkeeper. Having spent three seasons in the 'A' team and reserve side, he made his league debut, replacing the injured Tony Waiters, against Fulham on 29 January 1966 and with Waiters still incapacitated he retained the spot for the game with Tottenham Hotspur a week later. Taylor did his long-term chances no harm as both games ended in a 0-0 draw with the headline 'A Taylor-made Draw' appropriately covering the report of the first game with a further comment "part-time keeper makes sure of a point for Blackpool". He later became the club's regular goalkeeper and made 106 appearances before moving to Southport.

A PROVEN GOALSCORER

When 35-year-old David Cross joined Blackpool for a pre-season trial, having been released by Bury, he had 194 league goals to his name with his previous ten clubs. He played two pre-season friendly games for Blackpool and impressed manager Sam Ellis to such a degree that he offered Cross a contract. However, Cross rejected the deal, choosing to accept a lucrative one-year deal with Limassol of Cyprus.

'ZOOM'

Zambia's leading footballer, playing with Mufulira Wanderers and captaining the national side, 29-year-old Samuel 'Zoom' Ndhlovu spent almost a month with Blackpool in August 1966. Manager Ronnie Suart said, "He will be joining in the training sessions and the coaching and he will be here until about 31 August." He arrived in town in early August, having watched some of the World Cup games, and watched Blackpool reserves defeat Preston North End reserves 2-1 at Bloomfield Road in a pre-season friendly game on 8 August. Ndhlovu was in England on an FA coaching course in Durham after which he returned to his country to continue his career in which he went on to coach the Zambian national side on three separate occasions.

THROUGH THE TURNSTILES

At the end of the 2001/02 season attendances at Bloomfield Road had increased by 28.6% as compared to 2000/01. Only at Brentford, 44.5%, and Cardiff City, 57.3%, was support increased by a larger percentage so it proved chairman Karl Oyston's point that supporters would return when they were given a stadium to be proud of. In 2000/01 the average attendance over the season had been 4,457 while in 2001/02 it was 5,730, a figure boosted by the crowds that flocked to the ground for the Huddersfield game, when the new West Stand was officially opened, and games thereafter. The chairman commented, "We estimated that the crowds would level out just short of 8,000 and I think our estimate was about right."

RAZZMATAZZ A-PLENTY

It was bands, beauty queens and souvenir rock when Wrexham came to Bloomfield Road on 11 May 1985 because by then Blackpool had already been guaranteed promotion from Division Four and were unbeaten in 12 games, six won and six drawn. A crowd of 6,093 turned up to see the bands oompah but there was no such thing in Blackpool's play with the only saving grace being Eamonn O'Keefe's shooting power. Even he could not put the ball in the net but neither could Wrexham so honours were even with a 0-0 draw and Blackpool extended their unbeaten run to 13 games, which was the then current best in British football, for the only other side in with a shout, Everton, lost that day.

THE REAL DEAL

Blackpool were the first British team to appear in the Costa Del Sol tournament at Malaga on 14 August 1963 but they were unfortunate in that firstly they met the mighty Real Madrid, who had won the European Cup five years in succession from 1956 to 1960. Prior to the game the Malaga weekly sports newspaper *Rosaleda* misguidedly stated, "They finished third in the league last season, battling all the way with the top two. Their ground is in Bloomfield Road and has an official capacity of 48,000. Their players enjoy a world-wide reputation for good behaviour on the playing field where, apart from their skill and quality, they captivate everybody with the excellent sportsmanship they show." Blackpool had actually finished 13th in the First Division table in the 1962/63 season and their ground capacity was well short of the quoted figure. The *Rosaleda* reporter went on to outline profiles of some of the players one of which read, "Ball, midfield, the baby of the side, only 18 years of age, skilful and with a great future." At least the reporter got that right! He went on to say "There is no doubt that Blackpool will not be easy opponents and that if Real Madrid wish to get to the final – let nobody doubt it – they will first of all have a tricky task, which may just leave them in the lurch." That was not to be the case as Real Madrid, with many of their famous internationals on show, were 4-0 in front at half-time with the goals coming from Ruiz, Amancio, Di Stefano and Gento. Ray Charnley did pull one back for Blackpool but as the local press stated in its headline over three lines of text, REAL MADRID TOO GOOD FOR BLACKPOOL.

ON THE FARM

Brian Caine had an unenviable job when he signed for Blackpool for the 1955/56 season; he was to be the number two to goalkeeper George Farm, who rarely missed a game. Caine remained at the club for four seasons, playing 95 times in the Central League, but he made only one first-team appearance when Farm reported unfit for the game against Bolton Wanderers on 28 December 1957. He was unlucky enough to concede a Jimmy Armfield own goal after nine minutes and Blackpool never recovered, losing 3-2.

A CRICKETING FOOTBALLER

When Lawrence Cook signed for Blackpool in August 1904 he was the groundsman and junior professional at Lytham Cricket Club and had previously played for Nelson Cricket Club. Although a centre forward, he played his nine games for Blackpool on the right wing and then departed for Preston North End at the end of the season. He played only three games for Preston but in 1907 he made his debut for Lancashire County Cricket Club and went on to play 203 matches for the county, scoring 2,051 runs at an average of 12.28 and taking 821 wickets at an average of 21.36. He took 100 wickets in a season on three occasions, his best return being 156 wickets at an average of 14.88 in 1920.

SURPLUS TO REQUIREMENTS

Having played just one league game for Blackpool, full-back Alan Burrows was given a free transfer on 10 March 1961 following the decision to abolish the maximum wage for players. Ironically he had earlier attended the players' meeting in Manchester along with team-mates Stan Matthews and Bill Perry and had voted for the abolition of the maximum wage. He commented on the decision with "There was no doubt we were among the first casualties after our union's insistence on the abolition of the maximum wage, freedom to negotiate contracts and other things." However he went on to establish a successful career in Rhodesia where he played for Salisbury and City of Lusaka, winning the Rhodesia Cup with the latter side when, from an unaccustomed centre forward position, he scored the winning goal in his side's 3-2 victory. He was so successful that he also became a Rhodesian international, winning three caps for his adopted country.

A SHORT TOUR

Blackpool took 15 players on their two-match tour of Ireland in April 1947. A few hours after arriving they defeated Distillery 5-2 in a benefit match at Grosvenor Park, Belfast with goals from Stan Mortensen, two, George Dick, two and Jimmy McIntosh. After spending Saturday as guests of the Irish FA at the Irish Cup Final and Sunday sightseeing at Portrush, they lost 1-0 to Coleraine despite playing what the Irish press described as "exhibition football".

A CULTURAL TOUR

Blackpool embarked on a southern tour in January 1894 with games arranged against Millwall Athletic, Woolwich Arsenal and Sheppey United. The team, prematurely dubbed by the southerners as "the Lancashire League champions", left Central Station on Friday afternoon 26 January and a weary journey saw them reach London at 9.30 that evening, two and a half hours later than expected. An omnibus was taken to Ye Olde Belle Hotel in St Paul's Churchyard, Ludgate Hill and after supper it was straight to bed. Saturday morning was spent at St Paul's Cathedral, the Houses of Parliament and Westminster Abbey before dinner was taken prior to the trip to Millwall. Light refreshments were then taken at The George Hotel where the players met an ex-Blackpool player, George Challenor, who worked in the city. The team received a tremendous reception when at the East Ferry Road ground and everyone was happy when the game was drawn 2-2, Blackpool's goals coming from 'Gyp' Cookson and Billy Marsden. That evening was spent at Daly's Theatre in Leicester Square where Shakespeare's *Twelfth Night* was having a successful run. Sunday was spent sightseeing in the West End and Piccadilly, Monday morning at the Inns of Court, the Temple and the Tower of London before the trip from Cannon Street station to Woolwich. Posters in the streets around the ground advertised Blackpool, the leaders of the Lancashire League and 2,000 enthusiastic spectators welcomed the team onto the field. Marsden and Tommy Wilkinson scored goals but even so Arsenal won 5-2 but "after a hearty tea" the players brushed off their defeat with a visit to the Haymarket Theatre to see The Charlatans. On Tuesday morning a bus was taken to the National Gallery where many of the 1,170 exhibits were viewed before the trip to Sheppey. Posters in the Isle were even more eulogistic than at Woolwich as they declaimed GREAT MATCH AT SHEPPEY First visit of the Blackpool Football Club. Sheppey United v Blackpool (Champions of the Lancashire League). And Blackpool did not disappoint, showing their superiority with a resounding 4-0 victory with the goals coming from Cookson, two, Billy Porter and 'Squash' Stirzaker. The Alhambra was visited on Tuesday evening and on Wednesday in "a dirty, disagreeable drizzle" the team visited the British Museum followed by the Gaiety Theatre in the evening when a Blackpool girl, Miss Cissy Loftos, was appearing. London was left at 11.30am on Thursday and an exhausted team arrived back in Blackpool at eight o'clock that night.

CHANGING TRAINS

Owing to delays on the railway the Leeds United reserve team had to change on the train and walk in their football strip to Bloomfield Road for their Central League match with Blackpool reserves on 1 September 1923. It did them no harm as they defeated Blackpool 2-1.

UNLUCKY RAY

One of Blackpool's best ever bargains was centre forward Ray Charnley who was signed for just £775 from Morecambe in May 1957. Once he secured a regular first-team place, in January 1958, he led the Blackpool goalscorers in seven of the nine seasons that he was a regular and overall scored 222 goals. However England honours continued to elude him even though the national press clamoured for his inclusion in the side. There was universal press uproar in November 1961 when Ray Crawford of Ipswich Town was picked for England ahead of him and on hearing of Crawford's selection, Blackpool manager Ronnie Suart commented, "I am surprised to hear that Crawford has taken preference over Charnley whom I consider to be better equipped for the England job. When will the selectors give this grand player a break?" The answer to Suart's question was to come almost 12 months later when Charnley was selected for his country against France at Hillsborough in the European Nations Cup on 3 October 1962. It was "an unconvincing display" by England who drew 1-1 with Charnley being fouled for the penalty from which Ron Flowers equalised. It was to be Charnley's only international cap.

PREMATURE END

With Blackpool losing 9-1 at Small Heath (later Birmingham City) on 2 March 1901, the referee mistakenly blew his whistle for full-time and took the players off the field four minutes early. When he realised his mistake, "with many of the players partially dressed" and "much to their disgust" he took the players back out to complete the 90 minutes. And to add insult to injury, Small Heath, in front of an empty ground as all the spectators had left, added another goal to make the final score an embarrassing 10-1.

A STARTLING SUCCESS

Goalkeeper Jack Hacking was signed by Blackpool from Grimshaw Park Co-operative, Blackburn in January 1920 but due mainly to the presence of Harry Mingay he did not have an extended run in the league side until the back end of the 1923/24 season. He played a few games in 1924/25 but then Blackpool signed Len Crompton and once again he was relegated to the reserve side. At the end of the 1924/25 season, after playing only 33 games in five seasons, Blackpool gave him a free transfer and he went into non-league football with Fleetwood before Oldham Athletic signed him for 1926/27. He quickly established a reputation with Oldham and, having won Football League honours in 1928, he won three England international caps in the 1928/29 season, playing against Scotland, Wales and Ireland.

ONE SHORT

It was perhaps no surprise that Blackpool lost their Lancashire League game 6-1 to Burslem Port Vale on 21 January 1899 for Alex Stuart missed the train and Blackpool had to play the whole game with ten men.

LATE KICK-OFF

Blackpool played Barcelona at Las Corts on 22 May 1957 and the game was scheduled to kick off at 10pm. However, the kick-off was delayed until 10.40pm, Blackpool's latest ever kick-off time. Firecrackers welcomed the Blackpool side into the arena and a cracking game ensued. It was 2-2 at half-time, Blackpool's goals coming from Ken Smith and Ernie Taylor, but late in the game Barcelona took a 3-2 lead. Blackpool fought back and with only a few minutes remaining 'Sandy' Harris scored the equaliser in the 3-3 draw.

EVANS ABOVE

Lorenzo Evans missed the train for Blackpool's trip to play Gainsborough Trinity on 19 April 1902 and the Seasiders had to play the game with ten men. Gainsborough, bottom of the table won 3-0, one of only four victories they had all season.

SIZE ISN'T EVERYTHING

Blackpool required at least one point to become champions of Division Two when they journeyed to the City Ground of Nottingham Forest on 3 May 1930. After a titanic struggle the game eventually ended in a 0-0 draw and the first celebrations, outside of the City Ground, were at Bloomfield Road. A crowd of 5,000 had been present to see the reserve side lose 3-1 to Huddersfield Town reserves, but the main focus was what was happening elsewhere. And the crowd lingered after the final whistle to await the result of the game against Forest and when it came through the fans gave a mighty cheer for their heroes. The journey home from Nottingham was by train and when it arrived at Kirkham, the stationmaster boarded it to inform the players that there was a huge crowd gathered at North Station to welcome them home. One of the players, more unassuming than the rest, said that he wanted to get off there and then and await another train so that he could avoid any fuss. But his team-mates persuaded the great Jimmy Hampson to remain with them and receive the adulation of the crowd. He duly did so and it took the players some considerable time to get away from the station after they departed the train. And it did not end there, for there was a civic reception at the Town Hall and 25,000 people gathered in Talbot Square as the players appeared one by one at the window of the mayor's parlour. They all received rapturous cheers, particularly Jimmy Hampson who had scored 45 league goals in 41 appearances, and one of the guests, First Lord of the Admiralty, the Rt Hon A V Alexander, met the players and said to Hampson, "Why, you don't look big enough to have scored all those goals!"

FANCY MEETING YOU HERE

Two players who signed for Blackpool on successive days and made their debuts for the club in the same game had previously made each other's acquaintance in very different circumstances. George Harrison, signed on 10 November 1931 from Preston North End, and Tommy Wilson, signed from Huddersfield Town on 11 November 1931, had fought together in World War I in the trenches at Rouville, Arras, in 1917. Their Blackpool debuts ended in a 2-1 defeat by Sheffield Wednesday.

CHRISTMAS CHEER

Blackpool played their first Christmas Day game in 1897 when they lost 3-2 to Newcastle United and they played on 25 December more often than not thereafter but the festive game that gave Blackpool supporters much pleasure was one that took place in 1958. It was the first time that Preston North End were the opponents and a crowd of 24,411 were present at Bloomfield Road to see Bill Perry give Blackpool the lead but Preston go into the break 2-1 in front. But two more goals from Perry and one from Jimmy Kelly in the second half gave Blackpool a convincing 4-2 victory. The Blackpool fans celebrated by singing, "We wish you a Merry Christmas" to their Preston counterparts! There was even more joy the following day as Blackpool went to Deepdale and in front of 36,450 spectators won 3-0 with two goals from Ray Charnley and one from Jimmy Kelly.

AND THEN THERE WERE 10

Blackpool's highest score in a competitive game is the 10-0 victory over Lanerossi Vicenza in the Anglo-Italian Cup competition on 10 June 1972. Micky Burns opened the scoring in the first minute and it was 4-0 at half-time as Alan Ainscow, two minutes, Alan Suddick, 15, and Glyn James, 31, hit the net. The six second half goals came in the space of 22 minutes as Lanerossi centre-half Stanzial scored an own goal after 49 minutes, Burns added two more, 58 and 60 minutes, Mick Hill scored two, 65 and 67 minutes, and Burns completed the scoring in the 71st minute. After Blackpool's seventh goal the Lanerossi goalkeeper Anzolin had apparently had enough for he simply walked off the field and substitute goalkeeper Bardin had to finish the game.

LOCAL BOY MADE GOOD

Blackpool-born George Wilson was signed by Blackpool as a promising amateur centre forward in December 1911. He was converted to centre half in September 1914 and later captained the side before he became Sheffield Wednesday's then record signing in March 1920. Two years after leaving Bloomfield Road he was captaining England and went on to win 12 caps. After five years at Hillsborough he played for Nelson until his retirement in 1930.

AND TOMORROW'S OPPONENTS ARE ...

Manager Steve McMahon was furious on 23 October 2003 when he discovered that a number of his players did not know who the following day's opponents were. He said that he expected his players to be fully aware of who they were facing and added, "I feel passionately about this. If players can't tell me who they are playing on the Saturday, then that is a sad indictment on football in this day and age. It's costing us. I'd be up all night, I'd know the danger players and what I needed to do to cope with them. I would certainly do my homework and I wouldn't need anybody else to tell me. I ask some of the players who they are playing against and they honestly don't know. It's true. For me, when you're a footballer you have to live and breathe football. You've got to know who you're playing against on the Saturday. I'm not just talking which team – I'm talking about individual players." Blackpool's players discovered they were playing Plymouth Argyle but it did not do them much good for they lost 1-0.

WORLD CUP POLE

Polish-born striker Adam Wolanin played some Central League and 'A' team football for Blackpool in the 1946/47 season while he was serving with the Polish Air Force. He emigrated to the United States in 1947 and went to live in Chicago where he played football for various Chicago teams, the Maroons, the Eagles and the Falcons. While with the Eagles he was selected for the United States World Cup squad in 1950 when one of the originally selected players, Ben McLaughlin, could not get time off work to go to the tournament in Brazil. And Wolanin made his international debut in the World Cup tournament at outside-right for his adopted country against Spain who defeated the United States 3-1. It was to be his only international appearance.

A YOUNG PAIRING

When 16-year-old David Bardsley made his Central League debut and partnered 16-year-old Colin Greenall in the centre of defence against Preston reserves on 3 March 1981, it was Blackpool's youngest ever pairing at that level. Both had good games but Preston won 1-0.

RELIEF

After 17 games without a goal, striker Mike Sheron finally opened his account in Blackpool's 1-0 LDV Vans triumph over Doncaster Rovers on 5 November 2003. He was set up by a Scott Taylor cross and had no difficulty in burying his close range header. He commented, "I think I'd have walked off if I had missed from there but I enjoyed it and it was superb to see the ball go in. I must admit I never expected to get to November without scoring but I kept believing in myself and the lads kept believing in me and it's great to get off the mark." It did, however, take him a further five games to score his first league goal and he finished the season with 11 goals in 50 appearances.

BY APPOINTMENT

The first time a member of the Royal family watched Blackpool play was on 27 April 1932 when the club was desperately fighting to avoid relegation. It was at St James' Park, Newcastle, and the Prince of Wales was present to see an exciting game drawn 2-2 with both Blackpool goals scored by Jimmy Hampson. The reason that the future King Edward VIII was present was that four days earlier Newcastle United had won the FA Cup by defeating Arsenal 2-1 with two goals from Allen and he was present to be introduced to and to congratulate the Newcastle team. However, he was also introduced to the opposition, so Blackpool's captain Eric Longden took the prince along the line of his men.

ANIMAL CAPERS!

Members of Blackpool's board met the mayor and town clerk in April 1930 to discuss the proposed formation of a company for a zoo and sports centre at Squires Gate. The mayor suggested that the football club move from Bloomfield Road and play on a well-equipped ground at Squires Gate at a rent of around £1,000 per annum. The immediate reaction of the directors was that Squires Gate was not in the Borough of Blackpool but they viewed the proposed site but thought "it could not be put in order for next season" so the proposal was rejected.

CUP TRAFFICKING

The draw for the second round of the FA Cup in 1906 paired Blackpool at home to Sheffield United and as the club were greatly in need of funds the view was "a considerable amount which must accrue from having to play Sheffield United in the next round will replenish the coffers of the Seasiders at a critical time". At the time of the draw Blackpool were still involved in a replay with Crystal Palace, which was again drawn and a second replay took place at Aston Villa's Aston Lower Grounds. There was a representative from Sheffield United at the game that Blackpool won 1-0 and he offered the Blackpool committee the opportunity to play the second round tie at Bramall Lane but "his terms were insignificantly small and were not entertained for a moment". Blackpool supporters obviously wanted the game played at Bloomfield Road but the committee, aware of the need for extra finance, were prepared to accept a good guarantee to move the game. No agreement had been reached by 27 January and the Football Association became concerned at what it considered "the buying and selling of Cup ties" and, noting the situation, there was every probability that it would "put a stop to this trafficking in Cup ties in the future". Blackpool eventually accepted a £250 guarantee or half the gross gate if receipts exceeded £500. The committee considered this a worthwhile deal, as they did not expect to take £250 if the game was played at home. On the day, Blackpool confounded the critics by defeating the First Division side 2-1 and the gate brought in £310, all of which prompted the *Daily Mail* correspondent to comment, "United have to reflect upon a loss of cash as well as prestige by their bargain." Many other nationals noted the situation and *The Athletic News* commented, "We strongly protest against this trafficking in grounds, as opposed to the spirit of the Cup system, as eliminating sport, and as unjust to loyal supporters of the smaller clubs. Blackpool have done a service to the game, and we only need now a resolution by the Council of the Football Association forbidding the sale of ground rights to keep the tourney on the right lines." The *Sheffield Independent* commented, "United, whom we all expected to sail serenely past Blackpool into the third round, suffered the indignity of absolute defeat on their own ground from a team holding a very lowly position in League football."

GET AHEAD, GET A HAT-TRICK

Alan Withers had played only 11 reserve games when he was selected for his league debut against Huddersfield Town on 18 November 1950 but he had proved his goalscoring ability with seven goals at that level. He continued his goalscoring exploits as he made a sensational debut with all three goals in Blackpool's 3-1 victory. He also went into the record books as the first player to score a hat-trick on his First Division debut. He kept his place in the side for five games and when scoring in a 4-4 draw with Arsenal on 9 December he was described as "that gay young poacher of goals"! Shortly afterwards Blackpool signed Allan Brown and Withers returned to the reserve side.

PILGRIMS PROGRESS

When Blackpool narrowly missed out on promotion from Division Two in 1976/77, manager Allan Brown reflected on two crucial games where points were lost. Four key points went begging to Plymouth Argyle, who were relegated to Division Three, and at season's end Brown commented with great regret, "We lost 2-0 at home and by the same score away."

STEELE'S THE NAME

With Blackpool having a goalkeeping crisis in September 1983 Simon Steele was signed on loan from Brighton and Hove Albion. Ironically Blackpool's third-string goalkeeper was also named Steele, Shaun of that ilk. Simon played three league games before being sent back to Brighton injured while Shaun only made the Central League side.

FLYING VISIT

When Dave Serella went on a month's loan to Irish part-timers Drogheda early in the 1983/84 season the Irish club flew him over each week and their supporters wondered where they had got the money to do such a thing with gates of only 2,000. It transpired that they had made plenty of money from their early season UEFA Cup clash with Spurs and had decided to use it to bring in some experienced league footballers to try to lift the club away from the bottom of their league. After his loan Serella returned to finish the season with Blackpool, who released him in May 1984.

HIS OWN MAN

When manager Steve McMahon made nine changes to the team to play high-flying Brentford at Bloomfield Road on 19 March 2002 he incurred the wrath of other Division Two promotion-chasing clubs. Brentford won 3-1 but McMahon commented, "We put out a team capable of getting a result but we didn't get it. Brentford turned us over. I think it was Brighton who complained that we put out a weakened team. But I've got to look at this football club, no one else. I've got to do what's best for the players here and what's best for me. I'm not going to start pleasing other people. I'm the manager and I'll please me not other managers."

FISHY BUSINESS

Prior to the start of the 1983/84 season newly signed striker Keith Mercer was hoping to add a third Division Four title to the two he had won at Watford and Southend United. Indeed, he was angling for success, having been a keen sea angler for many years and he introduced the hobby to a number of his Bloomfield Road team-mates. Mercer commented, "I've found sea angling is a marvellous way to get away from the pressures of football and completely relax. Hopefully it will help us achieve the success we want this season. It will certainly help with team spirit which is already marvellous."

HORSE POWER

In the early 1920s a horse-pulling roller was used on the Bloomfield Road pitch, which was regularly said to have "looked at its best".

A MOVEABLE STAND

The Motor Stand, which stood at the north end of the Bloomfield Road ground, was so called because it started life as a stand for spectators to view the motor car speed trials that were held on the New Promenade in 1904, 1905 and 1906. It was moved to Bloomfield Road on loan from the Corporation in October 1906 and was ready for the game with West Bromwich Albion on 10 November 1906. The football club eventually purchased it for £100 in June 1908 and it was covered by a roof in August 1911.

MID-TERM REPORT

With Blackpool in second place in Division Four, four points behind leaders York City, at the halfway stage of the 1983/84 season, manager Sam Ellis commented, "Our league position looks good. But we've got there more through effort than particularly consistent play up to now, and that consistency will have to come if we are to stay there. We are definitely short of a few goals. It's something we have been trying to put right in training, but which we haven't got right yet in our league games. We still have a long way to go but there are good signs. Not the least is that we now have money available for strengthening. In doing that we have to make sure we improve the quality as well as the numbers. In terms of effort, it will be difficult to better what we already have." Sadly Blackpool fell away in the second half of the season to finish in sixth place, ten points adrift of the promotion places and 29 points behind champions York City.

JUSTICE

Blackpool protested about a 2-0 defeat by the Manchester United reserve side in the Lancashire Combination in the early part of the 1906/07 season "because the referee did not turn up". As a consequence the two clubs agreed to play the game as a friendly game with the result not counting in the league competition. However, United eventually got the result to stand officially and Blackpool were far from happy. In the return game in December Blackpool had no first-team game and fielded a very strong reserve side and won 4-0!

FIRST-CLASS

After Mansfield Town had visited Bloomfield Road on 27 September 1983 one of their supporters, Mr A Faulkner, wrote to the club praising the facilities at Bloomfield Road and in particular the catering facilities. He wrote, "The staff were very polite, the prices very reasonable and the food and drinks very tasty, unlike the sludge they serve at other grounds. I would like to thank the whole staff for their excellent work and the overall welcome feel of the ground. It was a very enjoyable visit." And all that after his side had lost 2-0.

INSURANCE POLICY

Against Farnworth Standard on 21 April 1888 centre forward Billy Parkinson suffered "an ugly kick, accidentally administered" that caused him serious injury and it was said that he would be out of work for some time. Blackpool agreed to pay him one pound per week while he was convalescing but the incident caused the club to take out insurance for the players for the 1888/89 season with each player insured for 30 shillings per week "so long as he is unable to follow his employment".

CHAMPIONS

Despite losing their final game at Fairfield 4-0, Blackpool won the Lancashire League title for the first time in 1893/94 and when the players arrived back at Central Station they were hoisted shoulder high and carried to a waiting waggonette as the Volunteer Band struck up 'See the Conquering Heroes Come'. Then it was off to the Wellington Hotel where Alderman Bickerstaffe proposed "Success to the Blackpool Football Club" and said that he had never had any doubt that the team were going to win the championship after the previous season's near miss. He felt that Blackpool would have an even better side the following season to which captain Harry Stirzaker responded with the hope that it would not be the last time the club won the championship. After the speeches the players and officials, accompanied by the Fife and Drum and Volunteer Bands, retired to the club's headquarters, the Stanley Arms, to continue the celebrations.

A MEAGRE RETURN

Blackpool's gate receipts for the 1899/1900 Lancashire League season averaged £23 per game with the Easter clash with Stalybridge bringing in the most money, £61, and the game against Wigan bringing in the least, £6.

AND THE SUBSTITUTE IS ...

Adam Nowland made only 18 starts for Blackpool but he did appear in the league side 69 times, 51 of them were as a substitute, the most by any Blackpool player.

A SCOTTISH GOALSCORER

When Scotsman Ken Dawson joined Blackpool from Falkirk for a fee of £2,800 on 9 May 1938, not only was he one of the best outside-lefts in Scottish football he was also a proven goalscorer. He netted 48 goals as Falkirk gained promotion to Scottish Division One and in his first season in the top flight he scored 26 goals in 38 games. However, his career in England failed to match that north of the border as it was eight games before he scored his first goal in a 2-1 defeat by Derby County on 1 October 1938. And even though in a game against Sunderland "there were times during the first 45 minutes when Kenneth Dawson gave promise that he will yet be the forward that he was in Scotland," he failed to live up to his reputation. In his own words he became "a disillusioned young man" and wanted to return north of the border. Falkirk obliged and paid £1,750 after he had played 12 league games for Blackpool, scoring a solitary goal. He was an instant success at Falkirk and ended his career with a remarkable 285 goals from 385 games.

HANKY-PANKY

After a fracas at the Blackpool versus Fleetwood Rangers game at the Copse field, Fleetwood on 25 April 1893 Blackpool's Edward 'Pank' Parkinson was suspended by the Lancashire Football Association along with the other protagonist Thomas Pratt of Rangers. The incident resulted in a magistrates appearance and Pratt was fined 5s 6d [26p].

POSTPONED ...

Blackpool's third round FA Cup tie with Norwich City in 1962/63 was postponed 11 times due to the weather. It was eventually played on 4 March 1962. The game was drawn 1-1 with Norwich winning the replay 3-1.

UNTIMELY INJURY

Selected to play for England 'B' against Scotland 'B' on 6 February 1957, Dave Durie suffered an injury and was obliged to withdraw from the game. Durie had alerted the selectors when he scored four goals for an FA XI against the Army on 7 November 1956. Although he played further games for the FA, he did not get a call-up to the national side again.

BLACKPOOL PLAYERS REPORT BACK FOR TRAINING, JULY 1938 WITH KEN DAWSON FAR RIGHT OF THE BACK ROW.

BLUSHES SPARED

Scott Taylor spared Blackpool the ignominy of losing to the Isle of Man part-timers in that island's tournament on 25 July 2003 when he scored twice in the second half and sandwiched in between was a Mike Sheron goal that helped Blackpool to a 3-1 victory. The Isle of Man side had been leading 1-0 at the break and Taylor commented later, "It could have been embarrassing. When we went 1-0 down I thought, 'oh, no'. To be fair in the first half we played some nice football but we just couldn't break them down." He added, "When our first goal went in, I think their heads dropped a little bit and we got on top of them after that. It was an interesting team talk from the gaffer at half-time, the type you normally get when you come in 1-0 down! But it perked us up and it showed in the second half. We came out and were a lot more patient, kept the ball better and finished up with a nice win."

ON TRIAL ONLY

Goalscoring midfielder Ray McHale from Sheffield United joined Blackpool for a trial in the pre-season of 1983/84 even though he had one year of his contract to run at the Yorkshire club. He appeared in five pre-season friendly games for Blackpool and proved to be "a fine organiser in midfield and an excellent passer of the ball". Even so, Blackpool decided not to go ahead with a deal and allowed him to return to his parent club. In September 1983 he was still keen to join Blackpool even though he was in the first team at Sheffield but no deal took place and he later moved on to Swansea City.

GREAT EXPECTATIONS

When Blackpool met Derby County in the FA Cup first round on 13 January 1923 they were expected to win comfortably. But Derby triumphed 2-0 and immediately after the game their supporters were handing out memorial cards to their Blackpool counterparts. The card read, "It was a game of football/That two teams had to play;/Blackpool said 'We're sure to win',/But Derby said 'Nay, nay,/Our forwards are the very best/Our backs they are no worse',/As Blackpool found out to their cost/Before they were dispersed."

SHORT FARE

In the Division Two game against Luton Town on 30 April 1898 at the Athletics Ground the weather was so bad that the referee "wisely curtailed the game to the extent of 20 minutes". In front of a miserly 200 spectators Blackpool won 1-0 and gate receipts were "a few shillings over £4".

QUITE A TURN

Blackpool played Accrington, the holders of the Lancashire Senior Cup, on 1 May 1888 and lost the game 8-2 but the afternoon ended on a happier note for the 4,000 that had turned up to see the game and admire Blackpool's previously won Lancashire Junior Cup, which was on display with its red favours in front of the grandstand. The reason for the jollity was that after the game there was "a grand display of [roller] skating" by the three talented Wright brothers. The brothers were all goalkeepers in local football with the best known being Blackpool's goalkeeper 'Lal' Wright, who had kept goal in the final and who gave an exhibition of comic skating. Wright was quite a character because he also performed at the circus with elephants!

LIFE SAVER

While playing for Blackpool Jack Parkinson was a regular member of the Blackpool Lifeboat crew, a calling he continued after his playing career was over. His bravery was noted after he attended the stricken *Rosaleen* near Fairhaven in the lifeboat *Robert William* on 4 November 1911, just six weeks before his tragic death.

BLACKPOOL IN THE VAN

After a singular lack of success in the minor cup competitions over the years Blackpool won the LDV Vans Trophy by defeating Cambridge United 4-1 with goals from John Murphy, Chris Clarke, John Hills and Scott Taylor in front of 20,287 at the Millennium Stadium on 24 March 2002. After being knocked out in the second round by Crewe Alexandra in 2002/03, Blackpool were back at the Millennium Stadium to reclaim their trophy in 2003/04. On 21 March 2004 goals from Murphy and Danny Coid gave them a 2-0 victory over Southend United with 34,031 there to witness the game.

TWO SHORT

Blackpool played all the second half of their league game with Stockport County with only nine men as Bob Birket and 'Jubba' Hardman refused to turn out for the second half as conditions were swamp-like due to heavy and persistent rain. It was so heavy in the first half that the referee and the two captains "held a consultation with a view to discontinue play" but they decided to struggle on. When half-time arrived, the players, who had "enjoyed all the delights of a mud bath", trooped off "like drowned rats". When the second half was due to start the Blackpool players "politely but firmly declined to have anything more to do with the game". But after the referee had performed a "series of whistling solos", four of the hardier members of the Seasiders' team "plunged disconsolately into the swamp ready to face the worst". Three more players then followed their colleagues' lead and the game restarted with Blackpool fielding seven men. After five minutes' play, two more players joined the fray but Hardman and Birket simply refused to go out. In what were described as "conditions of pure farce" Blackpool went from 2-0 down to lose 4-0, much to the delight of the home supporters who found Blackpool's behaviour "unsportsmanlike".

NO TOPERS

When Blackpool travelled to Nelson for a Lancashire League fixture on 28 October 1893 both teams were undefeated and in recognition of Blackpool's success, Mr Hartley of the Nelson committee met them at the station and took them to the Bull Hotel for lunch. After dining the players made their way to the ground in pouring rain and consequently the pitch was a sea of mud with the 2,000 spectators "blissfully ignoring the fact that the moisture was permeating through the clothing to the skin". At half-time coffee was served to the Blackpool players in their dressing room but 'Gyp' Cookson deliberately knocked the pot over, remarking "How do you know what's in it?" Both teams remained undefeated after a 3-3 draw.

PERSONNEL TURNOVER

Between February 1978 and February 1981 Blackpool had four chairmen, six managers and 61 different players as the club plunged from Division Two to Division Four.

CONNED

Blackpool signed Scottish international Alfie Conn in March 1981 with high hopes as the player had won a European Cup winners' medal and Scottish league and cup medals with his previous clubs. However he managed only three games for Blackpool, completing only one, and the club released him.

OVER TO YOU

After regular penalty taker Stan Mortensen missed from the spot in the 1950/51 season he let it be known that he had no inclination to take them again. Tommy Garrett was therefore nominated but when he missed in the cup tie against Stockport County on 27 January 1951, the responsibility was handed over to Allan Brown whose penalty won the quarter-final tie against Fulham 1-0. Blackpool marched on to the cup final but Brown was injured so missed the game and Eddie Shimwell, who had scored from the spot at Wembley in 1948, was nominated for Wembley.

CUP RICHES

After Blackpool had lost 5-0 to Newcastle United in the third round of the FA Cup on 24 February 1906 the Seasiders' committee learned that they had earned £521 from the tie at St James' Park to which skipper 'Jonty' Scott said, "They could have had twice as many goals with pleasure if they'd pay us at the same rate – £100 a goal!" The cup run that season netted Blackpool over £1,000, a sum of which the *Athletic News* correspondent commented, "That is even better than a town's subscription to keep the club alive."

BAD TIMING

When Allan Brown was sacked as Blackpool manager on 6 February 1978, following successive home wins against Charlton Athletic, beaten 5-1, and Blackburn Rovers, beaten 5-2, the club were on the fringe of the promotion race. Thereafter they won only one of their last 15 games, scoring only 17 goals, and nosedived into Division Three for the first time in the club's history.

CHRISTMAS CAPERS

Rather than play the usual festive fixture against South Shore, because the two clubs had "a rancorous spirit" between them over the non-arranging of a benefit game for South Shore's Bob Wilson, Blackpool arranged a southern tour for the Christmas period of 1892. The party left on an excursion train from Central Station at 7.30pm on Christmas Day when "travelling in the train was anything but a pleasure for the night was intensely cold" and it was "only a little before seven o'clock the following morning that their destination was reached". The party stayed near St Paul's Cathedral at Ye Olde Belle Hotel and immediately on arrival "sat down to a splendid breakfast"; the landlord was later quoted as saying, "Those Blackpudlians had big appetites." On 27 December the party departed from Paddington for their first game at Marlow, where they dined and then went on to defeat the home side 2-1. The following day they played Woolwich Arsenal and drew 1-1. The rest of the time was, according to one player, "spent in gallivanting about", which included spending much time in the music halls at one of which the question was asked by other patrons as to who the fine body of men in good voice were! There was a lot of fog around during their stay and one player was reported as very nearly choking "with the fog and the bread that was supplied to them at meals" while another said that they had only one glimpse of daylight the whole time and that was at Great Marlow. The party left London to return on Wednesday evening, 28 December.

ONE OF THE FINEST

The contractors for the South Stand that was to be built in the close season of 1926 were Messrs Harry Peers & Co, constructional engineers of Bolton. It was almost ready for the opening match of the 1926/27 season when the comment was: "The new stand at the south end of the ground, when it is completed, will be one of the finest football stands in the country. It affords a splendid view of the full length of the ground, and will include dressing rooms, baths and offices for administrative purposes." The stand was 50 feet high and provided accommodation for 3,500 spectators and the overall cost of construction was £15,000.

DROUGHT BROKEN

When Blackpool defeated Preston North End 3-1 on 7 November 1925, it was their first win over their local rivals in 11 attempts dating back to 1901.

ABSENT WITHOUT LEAVE (AWOL)

Full-back Jack O'Donnell was the central figure in a sensational incident when he disappeared in December 1931. He had played in a 4-3 victory over Grimsby Town on 28 November and was selected for the side to play Bolton Wanderers on 5 December. However, he could not be found and Stan Ramsay had to take his place. After exhaustive enquiries it was discovered that O'Donnell was on board a Fleetwood trawler, the *Cremlyn*, bound for the fishing fields off the Outer Hebrides. He later explained his trip was undertaken inadvertently as he was visiting a friend when the trawler put out to sea! He did not return to the side until 2 January 1932. This was not the only time he went AWOL: he did not report for training after the August Bank Holiday in 1932 even though it was known that he was back in Blackpool after having paid a visit to Ireland and having visited friends in Liverpool. His landlady was asked about his whereabouts and whether he had gone on another trawler trip. She replied, "I don't think so. He told me he would never go on another trawler after his last experience." The directors took a dim view of his actions, suspended him indefinitely and, despite an appeal to the Football Association, he never played for Blackpool again.

NO DOGS

In January 1935 the Blackpool players were instructed that they must not attend greyhound race meetings and that disciplinary action would be taken against any player disregarding the warning!

SMART NECKWEAR

Men's outfitters W H Orry were given permission to sell the official Blackpool Football Club ties in October 1930. In addition Jimmy Hampson was given permission to work for the firm for eight hours one week and 12 hours the next week providing that there was no clash of interests with the football club.

A FINE FINISH

Blackpool won the final 13 home games of the 1990/91 season, results that helped to move the club from 18th place to a final fifth place finish.

REINSTATED

Striker Carl Richards, signed from Peterborough United for £25,000 in January 1990, was not happy at being substituted at half-time against Chester City on 24 April 1990 when Blackpool were losing 3-0. Colin Methven pulled a goal back in the second half but Blackpool lost 3-1 while the management did not appreciate Richards' reaction. Shortly afterwards Blackpool sacked him for what was called "a breach of discipline". However, a Football League Management Committee heard his case on 5 June 1990 and he was subsequently reinstated at Blackpool, who immediately, at the start of the 1990/91 season, loaned him out to Telford. He returned to Bloomfield Road and made 25 appearances for the club that season, scoring four goals. Blackpool released him in May 1992 after he had made 45 appearances and scored eight goals.

ABANDONED WITH INTENT

Blackpool were losing their third qualifying round FA Cup tie against Darwen 1-0 on 12 December 1896 when the game was abandoned after 40 minutes. Blackpool won the return game three days later 2-1 but the club benefited only to the tune of £28 from both games, as the expenses were "unusually heavy".

CHEAP LABOUR

In the 1898/99 season Blackpool secretary Bob Middleton was earning five shillings [25p] per week. However, at the end of the season the club was in such financial difficulties that he had not been paid for some time.

HARD LABOUR

Mr T Cummings was appointed groundsman at Bloomfield Road in March 1952 a weekly wage of £8 10s 0d [£8.50].

ONE COLOUR

Blackpool changed to an all-tangerine strip for the 1995/96 season. It had been tried out by the reserves in a game at Bloomfield Road against Newcastle United on 26 April 1995 when Blackpool lost 1-0.

A LATE STARTER

Centre forward Ken Smith made his league debut for Blackpool in a 2-0 defeat by Wolverhampton Wanderers on 15 January 1955 but, because of the presence of Stan Mortensen and Jackie Mudie, he did not return to league action for more than two years. But when he did return he did so with a bang as he scored a hat-trick in Blackpool's 3-1 victory over West Bromwich Albion on 3 April 1957. He also scored in the following game, a 2-1 defeat by Newcastle United but then played only two further games that season, and those at half-back. He made one more appearance at centre forward before he was transferred to Shrewsbury Town on 11 October 1957 for a fee of £3,000.

ATTRACTIVE VISITORS

In the 1950/51 season Blackpool were the most attractive visiting club in the Football League as they drew in an average of 47,686 for every away game. This put them top of the pile with Arsenal, attracting 43,379, in second place. And this trend continued, for the club was the second most attractive visiting club in the 1952/53 and 1953/54 seasons, headed on each occasion by Arsenal, and was then again the most attractive visiting side in the 1954/55 and 1955/56 seasons. In 1954/55 they averaged 40,604 to Wolverhampton Wanderers' 39,054 and in 1955/56 they pulled in an average of 42,594 as compared to second-placed Wolverhampton Wanderers' 36,116.

ALL PRESENT AND CORRECT

To show they were prepared to stand up and be counted after Blackpool had been confined to relegation to Division Four in 1980/81, all the Blackpool directors attended the final league game of the season at Exeter on 2 May 1981. Chairman Bob Morans commented, "We are not trying to hide and felt we should all be here for the last match." Blackpool lost the game 1-0.

ROYALTY RETURNS

Prince William was a spectator at the game against Wolverhampton Wanderers on 20 November 2010 while he was spending time on a friend's stag weekend in the north. The party visited the Pleasure Beach on the morning of the match and then Prince William watched Luke Varney score a wonderful goal and Marlon Harewood add another to give Blackpool a 2-0 victory.

A GOALKEEPER IN GLASSES

When goalkeeper James Mitchell signed for Blackpool as an amateur in March 1915 he was said to be "the one and only custodian to wear glasses" and he often played with a blue and white bandana tied around his head. He only played five league games for the Seasiders in the 1914/15 season but did reappear occasionally in wartime football between 1915/16 and 1918/19. He also played for the Great Britain team in the 1920 Olympic Games in Stockholm while still a master at Arnold House School, Blackpool. He joined Preston North End in October 1920 and was in the side that lost the 1922 FA Cup Final 1-0 to Huddersfield Town. In that FA Cup Final he played a part in a rule change in the game for when Billy Smith took the penalty that won the game Mitchell "danced about on the line and waved his arms around trying to distract the penalty-taker". The authorities did not care for Mitchell's antics and shortly afterwards changed the law so that goalkeepers had to keep still until the penalty was taken.

THE PHANTOM WHISTLER

Blackpool were well beaten by Arsenal at Highbury on 17 December 1955 but they did score a bizarre goal to make the final score 1-4. The game was in its final minute when Arsenal full back Dennis Evans heard the final whistle so he casually kicked the ball past his goalkeeper into the net. Unfortunately a member of the crowd had blown the whistle and the referee had no option but to award a goal!